An Introduction to

CORPORATE
GOVERNANCE

and the

SEC

K. Fred Skousen

Steven M. Glover

Douglas F. Prawitt

THOMSON

SOUTH-WESTERN

Australia · Canada · Mexico · Singapore · Spain · United Kingdom · United States

THOMSON

SOUTH-WESTERN

An Introduction to Corporate Governance and the SEC

K. Fred Skousen, Steven M. Glover, and Douglas F. Prawitt

VP/Editorial Director:
Jack W. Calhoun

Publisher:
Rob Dewey

Sr. Acquisitions Editor:
Sharon Oblinger

Developmental Editor:
Allison Rolfes

Marketing Manager:
Chip Kislack

Sr. Production Editor:
Elizabeth A. Shipp

Technology Project Editor:
Robin K. Browning

Manufacturing Coordinator:
Doug Wilke

Art Director and Cover Designer:
Anne Marie Rekow

Cover Image:
© PhotoDisc, Inc.

Printer:
Westgroup

Contents

Preface

In a free enterprise economy, such as is found in the United States, continued growth and stability require a healthy flow of capital from private and institutional investors to the managements of business enterprises. When a company sells its stocks or bonds to the public, the public acquires a valid interest in the proper use, or stewardship, over the company's resources. The outside investors essentially become "absentee owners," who turn over the day-to-day operation of the company to an executive management team. Effective corporate governance policies and procedures are necessary to ensure the management team is working in the best interest of the absentee owners and society as a whole.

Simply defined, corporate governance consists of all the people, processes, and activities implemented to help ensure the proper stewardship over a company's assets. Effective corporate governance allows management the freedom to successfully lead a company in earning adequate returns for the absentee owners, while mitigating incentives to commit fraud and reducing the information asymmetry between absentee owners and management. Good corporate governance creates a system that demands proper stewardship over invested capital and requires accountability for the financial condition and performance of the enterprise. As an important element, financial reporting provides an essential accountability link in the proper functioning of corporate governance processes.

This text focuses on those processes directly related to the regulatory authority and oversight of the Securities and Exchange Commission (SEC)—primarily those processes and activities that involve the gathering and reporting of financial information. The Securities and Exchange Commission was established in 1934 in an effort to foster honest and open securities markets. Congress, in establishing the SEC, gave broad powers to the Commission to regulate securities and to ensure proper financial reporting and disclosure by American businesses.

The importance of the SEC and its dealings with the business community in general and the accounting profession in particular is, in the view of the authors, unquestionable. Accounting and financial periodicals frequently carry announcements of new accounting or disclosure rules or of the liability of an accountant or business executive under the Securities Acts. Many accounting, legal, and consulting firms derive a major part of their revenues from activities directly or indirectly related to the SEC. For accountants, these activities range from the certification of financial statements used in registrations under the various Securities Acts to the giving of advice on the applicability of different provisions of the Acts.

The purpose of this book, in a narrow sense, is to acquaint the reader with the nature, origin, and workings of the SEC, particularly as related to financial reporting. In a broader sense, this book deals with the informational needs and requirements relative to the capital markets. Hopefully, the reader will be able to see the relationship between investment decisions (by both investors and managers), capital markets regulation by the SEC, the effective functioning of corporate governance processes, and the role of the accountant and business executive relative to each.

The book is structured to accomplish these purposes. The first chapter gives an overview of the elements of effective corporate governance and the SEC's role in overseeing the financial reporting element. Chapter 2 offers an historical background to securities legislation in the United States and explains the structure and work of the SEC. Chapter 3 examines the legal framework of the SEC, with a brief explanation of each major Act administered by the Commission. Chapter 4 focuses on the SEC's registration process and reporting requirements, primarily under the 1933 and 1934 Acts. A brief tutorial for researching SEC accounting-related documents and registering online through EDGAR is also offered in appendices to this chapter. An analysis of reports presented to shareholders and those submitted to the SEC is given in Chapter 5. Actual examples are presented to highlight disclosure requirements. The final chapter looks at the extensive interaction between the SEC and the business community, focusing on the SEC's influence on financial reporting, auditing, and corporate governance practices.

In view of the impact of the SEC on business and the accounting profession, it is unfortunate that so little attention is given to the subject in typical business and accounting curricula. Some lengthy technical books on the subjects covered in this text are used by legal and accounting professionals. This introductory text attempts to summarize detail and to synthesize technicalities in a readable, useful manner for busy professionals as well as accounting and business students. Hopefully, this book will fill a need for a brief but substantial introduction to the SEC and its central role in promoting transparent information, effective corporate governance, and fiscal accountability.

Although intended primarily for busy professionals wanting an introduction to the SEC or as a supplement to intermediate college finance, accounting, or auditing courses, this book can easily be used in other settings to provide an overview of the SEC and its importance to business in general. This is especially needed in accounting and legal firms' training programs, as well as in graduate accounting or MBA programs where such exposure has not been provided previously. The book should establish a basis for further study and research into the separate topics described herein.

This book has benefited from the efforts of many people. Personal gratitude and the principle of full and fair disclosure require that we acknowledge these contributions collectively, if not individually. Special recognition is given to Professor Tatsuto Fujii, visiting Fulbright scholar from Tohoku Gakuin University, for his assistance with the fifth edition, and to J. Kent Millington and Michelle Lowry, who assisted significantly in the research and preparation of the first and sixth editions, respectively. We also recognize the capable research assistance of Joel Cowden, Jason Eldredge, McKay Marriott, Jason Smith, and David Wood in preparing the sixth edition. We are grateful to Professors Paul B. W. Miller, Steven A. Zeff, and Tom Weirich for specific suggestions that have been incorporated into various editions. Finally, we are grateful to numerous students and colleagues and to our families for their encouragement and assistance while writing and revising this book. Notwithstanding the involvement of others, the responsibility for any deficiencies in this book must be assumed solely by the authors.

K. Fred Skousen
Steven M. Glover
Douglas F. Prawitt
Brigham Young University

1

An Overview of Corporate Governance

PROSPERITY AND GREED

In the post-war 1920s, the United States enjoyed economic prosperity, and Americans searched for ways to participate in the booming economy. Although the stock markets operated largely without oversight or regulation, significant returns on investments and the possibility of climbing from "rags to riches" enticed more than 20 million investors to place their money, and their trust, in the stock market. For nearly a decade, consistent returns created a false sense of security for investors.

Preying upon the inflated trust of investors, numerous cases of securities fraud helped lead to the stock market crash in October of 1929. The market's value continued to plummet for the following three years, eventually bottoming out at a $15 billion market value, only 17 percent of the market's height earlier in the autumn of 1929. American investors lost billions of dollars as well as their confidence in the stock market. The fraud, deceit, and excesses of the 1920s were arguably major factors leading to the Great Depression.

Recognizing the need to restore investor confidence in public companies and in the stock markets, the United States Congress passed the Securities Act of 1933 and the Securities Exchange Act of 1934. The purpose of these acts was to help ensure the integrity and reliability of information provided to investors.

The Securities and Exchange Commission (SEC) was created in 1934 to enforce the newly passed Securities Acts. The SEC was given the authority and responsibility to protect investors from misleading information and to ensure the integrity of the securities exchange markets. Under the watchful eye of the SEC, investor confidence was slowly restored, and American investors eventually returned to the stock markets with renewed confidence and increased awareness of potential risks.

The SEC played an important role in improving the reliability of information used by investors, and despite periodic downturns, the stock market was seen as a relatively secure and lucrative investment for more than 50 years. In the 1990s, the introduction of exciting new technologies, such as the Internet and wireless applications, helped usher in a new era of "irrational exuberance." Technology startups found that market participants would provide capital to nearly any company that had a "dot.com" in the title. Price-to-earnings ratios grew to more than double their historical averages. Years of prosperity and the seemingly instant creation of huge sums of wealth for high-tech entrepreneurs and investors created a speculative greed that fueled inflated expectations. Investors were insufficiently skeptical and ignored periodic suggestions that the white-hot market activity could represent a market bubble rather than what many saw as a fundamental shift in the economy. This expectation of continued prosperity coupled with widespread speculation regarding the advent of the "new economy" created an opportunity for scandals similar to those that led up to the stock market crash of 1929.

In 1985, what later became known as one of the nation's most recognizable cases of greed and shame began when two relatively unknown companies, Houston Natural Gas and InterNorth, merged to form Enron. In an industry facing deregulation, newly introduced competition and a changing business environment threatened the young company. Recognizing the need for a new business strategy, management made a radical move: It repositioned Enron from an oil and gas retailer to an energy wholesaler that profited largely by bringing buyers and sellers together.

This radical change was immediately successful, prompting management to attempt to duplicate their new strategy in previously untapped markets and with a variety of products. For example, Enron created online or "virtual" markets to buy and sell hundreds of products including such items as electricity, natural gas, market research, training, hedges, futures, and eventually even Internet broadband.[1] Through this aggressive maneuvering, Enron became one of the largest public companies in the United States. These early successes were accompanied by increasing profits, stock prices, credit ratings, and public expectations.

As management continually strove to exceed rising expectations without compromising the public's perception of the company, aggressive, risk-laden ventures were encouraged. Unfortunately, many of the high-risk ventures turned sour, and the company turned to increasingly aggressive and eventually, improper accounting methods to conceal the losses and maintain a strong public image. For example, Enron reported revenue of over $7 billion for sophisticated transactions based on complex energy forecasting models that would not yield cash flows for more than ten years in the future. Shortly after bankruptcy proceedings began, it was learned that the value of these transactions had dropped to $1.2 billion. Enron executives had tweaked the forecasting assumptions in order to create higher revenues and to satisfy investor expectations. Enron was also expert at selling underperforming assets (e.g., a money-losing electrical power plant project in India) to "outside" investors for big profits. Thus, the transactions not only removed underperforming assets from Enron's books, but the company was also able to record sales and profits. The misleading part of these transactions was that Enron would fund and provide guarantees to the "outside" investors buying the assets. In the end, Enron was essentially selling underperforming assets to itself for more than the company had originally paid for them, thus reporting large, but fictitious, profits.

Disguising the losses led to an increasingly weakened financial position; however, the external auditors, who were also employed as the company's internal auditors, failed to adequately identify and challenge the improper accounting practices. In hindsight, it appears that the external audit firm,

---

1. Larry Downes, "Don't Cry for New Economy," *USA Today,* 23 May 2001. Accessed 18 Feb. 2004. <http://www.usatoday.com/news/opinion/2001-05-23-ncguest2.htm>.

Arthur Andersen, LLP, lacked sufficient objectivity in evaluating Enron's accounting methods. The lack of independence was allegedly due to conflicts of interest arising because Andersen served as both the internal and external auditor and the fact that Andersen was paid tens of millions of dollars in separate consulting fees amounting to more than the fee for the external audit itself. Regardless of the cause, Andersen failed to disclose and rectify the vast extent of Enron's improper accounting. Even though the audit committee went through the motions of inquiring of the external auditor regarding its independence, the committee failed to adequately evaluate the relationship between the auditor and the company.[2] Furthermore, the board of directors did not function independently from management since the chairman of the board also served as Chief Executive Officer (CEO) from 1986 to 2002.[3]

As a result of the deception accompanied by material failures in corporate governance, the public remained unaware of the impending downfall of one of America's most respected companies. For more than three years, many investors and lenders were misled by financial statements that presented Enron as a solvent profit leader in the industry, and they continued to funnel billions of dollars into a company on the brink of financial disaster.

The true financial condition of the company could not be concealed indefinitely. As executives resigned and employees began to come forward to question the company's accounting practices and dubious partnerships, the company's numerous problems began to come to light. In October of 2001, Enron reported its first quarterly loss. In response to the startling news and a flurry of questions from outside analysts and investment firms, the SEC launched an investigation into the company's accounting practices.

In an effort to restore confidence, top company officials held numerous conferences with analysts and investors; however, company executives became defensive as the analysts and investors pleaded that the company be more forthcoming about its operations. Shortly thereafter, under increasing pressure from employees, analysts, regulators, and the financial press, the company released earnings restatements for previous years disclosing

---

2. <http://www.wsws.org>
3. His term was interrupted for a six-month period in 2001, when he relinquished the CEO title.

billions of dollars in overstated earnings and previously undisclosed debt obligations.[4]

In the aftermath of Enron's collapse, numerous investigations were launched to identify the nature and extent of accounting improprieties and fraudulent actions taken by management. In addition to identifying the problems with Enron, these ongoing investigations focused the attention and efforts of regulators, including the SEC, on improving corporate governance.

Shortly after the Enron scandal, other scandals involving corporate giants (Tyco, WorldCom, Xerox, Adelphia, Ahold, etc.), brokerage firms (e.g., Merrill Lynch), stock exchanges (e.g., the New York Stock Exchange), large public accounting firms (e.g., Arthur Andersen, Deloitte, Ernst & Young, KPMG, and PricewaterhouseCoopers) and managers of mutual funds (e.g., Piper Jaffray) were uncovered. The Enron scandal alone weakened investor confidence in the stock market, but the subsequent series of scandals caused many investors to doubt the integrity of the entire system of public ownership and accountability.

Congress was again under pressure to restore public confidence through legislation, passing the enormously consequential *Sarbanes-Oxley Public Company Accounting Reform and Investor Protection Act* in July 2002. Similar to the impact of the Securities Acts of 1933 and 1934, the Sarbanes-Oxley Act started a process of broad reform in corporate governance practices that would affect the duties and practices of public companies, financial analysts, external auditors, and securities exchange markets. Corporate governance is affected by many aspects of the Sarbanes-Oxley Act and especially by Title III—*Corporate Responsibility*.

CORPORATE GOVERNANCE DEFINED

Securities exchange markets exist so that companies can raise the investment capital necessary to expand to new markets, to finance expensive research, and to fund the buildings, technology, and equipment necessary to deliver a product to market. Managers and entrepreneurs with the vision and expertise to run a successful business typically do not have sufficient

---

4. Arthur L. Berkowitz, *Enron: A Professional's Guide to the Events, Ethical Issues and Proposed Reforms* (CCH, Incorporated, 2002).

financial resources to start or support the business. Furthermore, the capital needs of companies often exceed the resources or risk preferences of any individual or small group of investors. A capital market allows a company to sell small pieces of ownership (i.e., stocks) or to disaggregate borrowed funds into small loans (i.e., bonds) so that vast amounts of capital can be raised from a collection of investors and creditors. Investors and creditors participate in the public securities exchange markets because they believe they can earn a better risk-adjusted return than if they pursued other investment options. A "Public Company," therefore, is a company that sells its stocks or bonds to the public, giving the public a valid interest in the proper use, or stewardship, over the company's resources. The result of *going public* is that the outside investors become "absentee owners," as they are absent from the day-to-day operations of the company. Instead, absentee owners turn over the day-to-day operation of the company to an executive management team. Public companies are organized as **corporations,** so in the remainder of this book the terms "company" and "corporation" are used interchangeably.

Because executive management is involved in every aspect of the business from past performance to future plans and prospects, the knowledge it possesses far exceeds the information available to the absentee owners. This imbalance or asymmetry in the quantity and quality of information places management in a position where greed and self-interest can lead it to misrepresent the true performance and condition of the enterprise. Members of management have incentives to misrepresent because the returns to them can be enormous if they can successfully overstate the value of the company to absentee owners and other marketplace participants. During the stock market bubble of the late 1990s, it was commonplace for executives to receive compensation valued in the tens or even hundreds of millions of dollars. The bulk of this compensation came in the form of stock, which was in some cases overvalued due to the misrepresentations executives had made to the marketplace through financial statements or other communications. Adequate corporate governance policies and procedures are necessary to ensure the management team is working in the best interest of the absentee owners and society as a whole. For example, greed, unchecked by adequate corporate governance practices, drove Enron executives to cash in millions of dollars worth of fraudulently inflated stock just before the company collapsed.[5]

---

5. Ibid.

Simply defined, **corporate governance** consists of all the people, processes, and activities in place to help ensure the proper stewardship over a company's assets. Corporate governance is the implementation and execution of processes to ensure that those managing a company properly utilize their time, talents, and the available resources in the best interest of absentee owners. These processes include all aspects of a company's performance including risk management, operational and marketing strategies, internal control, conformance with applicable laws and regulations, public relations, communication, and financial reporting. Effective corporate governance allows management freedom to successfully lead a company to earn adequate returns for the absentee owners, while mitigating incentives to commit fraud and reducing the information asymmetry between absentee owners and management. Good corporate governance creates a system that demands proper stewardship over invested capital and faithfully reports the economic condition and performance of the enterprise.

Although corporate governance extends to all facets of operations of a public company, this text focuses on those processes directly related to the regulatory authority and oversight of the Securities and Exchange Commission (SEC)—primarily processes and activities that involve the gathering and reporting of financial information.

SEC AND CORPORATE GOVERNANCE MODEL

There are many components and key players within the corporate governance model. These players interact on various levels to help ensure the objectives of corporate governance are met. Some players in the model have more involved roles than others, but each participant in corporate governance is important to the overall success of the entire model.

The SEC's Role in Corporate Governance

As mentioned previously, the United States Congress created the Securities and Exchange Commission in response to numerous securities frauds committed in the 1920s and early 1930s. The SEC was created to oversee and regulate companies whose shares are traded publicly through exchange markets. The SEC's realm of authority and oversight reaches into many aspects of corporate governance, but its main focus is to protect investors from misinformation and maintain the integrity of exchange markets.

Exhibit 1-1: The SEC and Corporate Governance

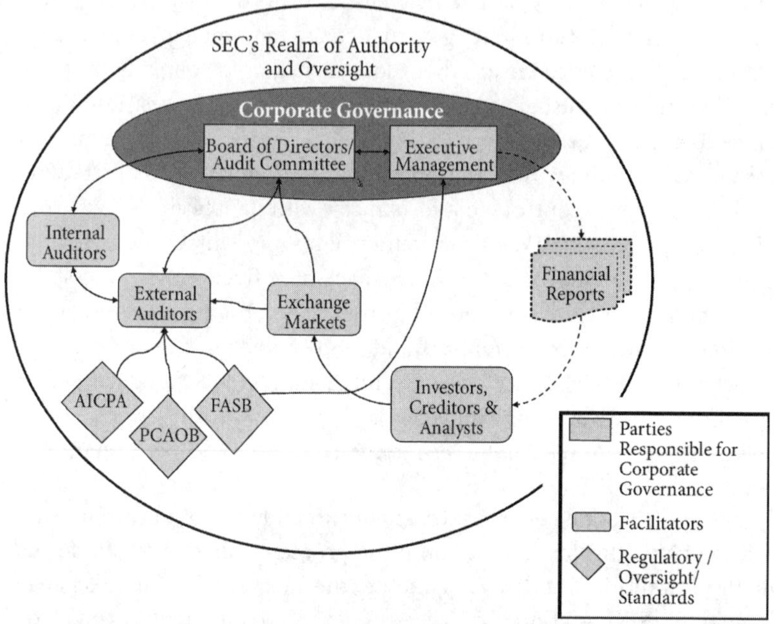

The policing role played by the SEC through the enforcement of laws and regulations has far-reaching effects into the function of corporate governance. In light of recent accounting scandals, Congress has given the SEC authority to expand its oversight of public companies by imposing new requirements that provide additional guidance as to the preparation and dissemination of financial information. By taking new measures to improve corporate governance, the SEC has arguably made progress in restoring investor confidence.

The remainder of this chapter focuses in more detail on the major players in corporate governance over which the SEC has responsibility or influence. As illustrated in Exhibit 1-1, these parties can be grouped into three categories—those primarily responsible for *executing* appropriate corporate governance practices, those that *facilitate* effective corporate governance, and those that have *regulatory or oversight* responsibilities, such as standard setters.

Parties Responsible for Corporate Governance

Executive management, the **board of directors**, and the **audit committee** are the parties principally responsible for corporate governance. Each of these groups, described in more detail below, is internal to the corporation. This is indicated in Exhibit 1-1 by the shaded oval labeled "corporate governance."

Executive Management.   Investors and creditors (the absentee owners of a public company) delegate the everyday operations and activities of the company to executive management. Management has the responsibility to act in the best interest of the absentee owners when considering corporate activities and policies.

Traditionally, members of executive management have been rewarded with performance-based compensation and bonuses that have occasionally led members of management to mask financial troubles within a company in order to cash in on stock options or other performance-based compensation. An example of this behavior is evident in the months leading to the downfall of Enron. In August 2001, just three months prior to the implosion of the company, the CEO sold 93,000 shares for $2 million, while encouraging employees to purchase more shares because Enron's stock was "undervalued." Less than three months later, company employees and millions of other shareholders watched as Enron's stock price fell to nearly zero, and their retirement savings and other investments in Enron went up in smoke.[6]

In an attempt to strengthen the accountability of members of management, Congress passed the Sarbanes-Oxley Act of 2002, which prescribes new, more stringent regulations for members of executive management. For example, today, under the threat of criminal punishment, the CEO and the Chief Financial Officer (CFO) must personally certify the accuracy of the financial statements and related disclosures filed with the SEC. These executives must also certify that the internal processes used to gather and verify the information are adequately designed and operating. If the information filed with the SEC is determined to contain false or misleading information, company executives who certified the information with the knowledge that it contained false or misleading information face the possibility of up to 20 years in prison. Certifying executives can also be forced to reimburse all profits gained from performance-based bonuses or

---

6. Ibid.

compensation along with all profits gained from the sale of company stock within the 12-month period prior to the filing of the erroneous statements.

Based on these new requirements and regulations, members of executive management are now more explicitly responsible for the information gathered and provided to investors. While the new certification requirements and the related penalties for the intent to deceive certainly enhance management's accountability, greed and dishonesty obviously cannot be removed through legislation. Thus, there will in all likelihood continue to be instances of misconduct and fraud in the future; however, it is hoped that the frequency and magnitude of the fraud can be reduced. Chapter 3 discusses the Sarbanes-Oxley Act in greater detail.

Board of Directors.   Boards are typically made up of 3 to 15 individuals that collectively have the expertise and experience to help direct a company. Board members are appointed directly by the shareholders to ensure management is acting in the best interest of the absentee owners. The board functions as an important advisor to management, but with the exception of hiring and firing top executives, it is not involved in the actual day-to-day operations of the company. Rather, the board lends its expertise to management in establishing the company's operating, financing, and marketing strategies. The board also consults with management regarding communications and financial reporting. When operating effectively, the board provides clear, objective guidance and oversees the performance and conduct of management.

Unfortunately, boards of directors do not always operate effectively. In fact, examination of past high-profile financial frauds (e.g., Enron, WorldCom, Tyco, Adelphia) reveals that the boards were inactive, lacked sufficient expertise, or were dominated by members of executive management. While it is relatively common to include members of management as part of the board because of their in-depth knowledge of the company and the industry, it is considered a best practice for a majority of the directors, including the chairperson, to be *independent*. Independent directors are paid for their services as directors, but they are not members of management and do not have other significant business relationships with the company.[7] Boards that are led or dominated by management are often

---

7. Among other restrictions, independent directors cannot be employees of the company and they cannot be a major supplier or customer.

perceived as just an extension of management, with little power to objectively direct or oversee the actions of management.

The lack of objective and effective boards contributed to the string of scandals that shook Wall Street in 2001–2003. The Tyco scandal is a prime example. In 2002, the SEC launched an investigation into improper accounting and company lending practices within Tyco, an international manufacturing and distribution company. The investigation uncovered enormous "loans" granted to corporate executives, most of which were never repaid. Most of the directors were unaware of the improper distribution of money because the loan practices were hidden by the chairman of the board, Dennis Kozlowski, who also happened to be Tyco's CEO and a primary recipient of the "loan" program. Because of the position Mr. Kozlowski held on the board of directors, he was able to filter information made available to other board members and to steer any curious board members away from further interest or investigation into the inappropriate activities.[8]

In response to various scandals involving corporate executives, many boards have replaced company executives serving as chairmen with independent directors. In addition to independent board members and better controls over executive compensation, boards are encouraged to carefully screen new members' qualifications and evaluate performance, establish anonymous "whistleblower" lines so that they are aware of complaints and potential wrongdoings, and to more effectively oversee the internal and external auditors.

In an attempt to strengthen boards of directors and corporate governance, exchange markets (e.g., the New York Stock Exchange, NYSE) started to require companies wishing to list on their exchanges to appoint independent directors, and at the writing of this book, they had issued proposals that would require a majority of independent directors.[9] The great irony of the NYSE-imposed rules is that in the midst of corporate scandals and revelations of executive excesses and ineffective boards, yet another scandal broke as a result of the NYSE's own lax corporate governance policies. The NYSE's board largely consisted of non-independent directors:

8. "Three Tyco Execs Indicted for Fraud," *CNN.com*, 12 Sep. 2002. Accessed 18 Feb. 2004 <http://edition.cnn.com/2002/BUSINESS/asia/09/12/us.tyco/>.
9. "Recommendations to the NYSE Board of Directors," New York Stock Exchange. Accessed 19 Feb. 2004 <http://www.nyse.com/pdfs/corp_recommendations_nyse.pdf>.

executives from the very firms that the Exchange regulates.[10] The NYSE is not a public company, but it serves the role of both a market maker and a quasi-regulator. As a regulator, the NYSE has the American public as its constituents; yet the integrity and objectivity of its own board of directors were not beyond reproach. In the spring of 2003, the SEC pressed the Exchange to review its corporate governance structure, and by September, the NYSE's ineffective corporate governance structure made headline news after the board approved the rich pay package of the exchange's chairman, Dick Grasso. Grasso was paid about $12 million in 2002, and $30 million in 2001. By comparison, the exchange industry average pay for head executives was about $1.3 million.[11] But Grasso's annual salary wasn't his only form of compensation. In September 2003, Grasso, the NYSE's longtime chairman and CEO, was ousted amid a public flap over his $187.5 million retirement package, to be paid in a lump sum prior to his retirement. At about the same time, the exchange's floor-trading firms, known as specialists, were the focus of a regulatory probe into whether they short-changed investors by at least $155 million over a three-year period.[12] In an attempt to restore public confidence, the NYSE board recruited Mr. John Reed, a former Citigroup Inc. chairman and co-CEO, who quickly moved to install a new board and remove the influence of Wall Street CEOs from matters such as compensation and regulation. The questionable nature of Grasso's compensation package is highlighted by the fact that Grasso's compensation was set by the board, and many on the board were executives for companies listed on the exchange.

Audit Committee.   An audit committee is a sub-committee of the board of directors. The audit committee is established by the board of directors for the purpose of overseeing the accounting and financial reporting processes as well as the internal and external audits.

The Sarbanes-Oxley Act, as well as some exchange markets, requires that members of the audit committee be independent of the company in order to ensure objectivity. The Act, and subsequent SEC rulings, also requires that at least one member of public company audit committees be a

---

10. Kate Kelly, et al. "Grasso Quits Amid Pay Controversy," *Wall Street Journal*. 18 Sep. 2003, sec A:1.

11. David Reilly, et al. "How Grasso's Pay was All-World," *Wall Street Journal*, 18 Sep. 2003, sec C: 12.

12. Susanne Craig and Kate Kelly, "NYSE Focuses on Grasso's Pay Deal," *Wall Street Journal*, 25 Nov. 2003, sec C: 13.

financial expert knowledgeable in financial statement analysis, audit procedures, and with an understanding of Generally Accepted Accounting Principles.[13]

The SEC mandated the use of audit committees in publicly held companies in the 1970s to ensure the integrity of the audit process, but audit committees were too often viewed as a necessary, but unimportant, evil; audit committees tended to meet only occasionally, usually following meetings of the full board. The SEC intended audit committees to be independent from management. The idea was to assure the integrity and independence of outside audits by encouraging auditors to be accountable to the audit committee instead of to management. For the most part, this did not happen. It was common for the committees to be comprised of and even chaired by members of management, and meetings were held jointly with members of the company's financial executives and the external auditor. "The failures of this last year [2002] are the failures in almost every case to confer that independence,"[14] argued former SEC chairman, Roderick M. Hills. Auditors essentially reported directly to company financial and operational executives, which probably made sense in a time when most audit committees delegated the hiring and firing of internal and external auditors to executive management. This lack of separation between auditors and management seriously jeopardized the ability of external auditors to take tough stands against aggressive managers and executives.

In the wake of the changes implemented in the post-Enron economy, the composition and duties of the audit committee are being reformed. Audit committee members are more informed about the operations and plans of the company. Effective audit committees now meet more frequently, and they meet in private with the external auditors. Meetings that were only allocated 30 minutes in the past can now take hours or even days. Audit committees of public companies can no longer delegate the hiring and firing of auditors to management because the Sarbanes-Oxley Act requires the audit committee to be directly responsible for appointing, compensating, and overseeing the audit firm's work. This includes resolving any disagreements over financial reporting between management and the

---

13. United States Securities and Exchange Commission, "Certification of Management Investment Company Shareholder Reports and Designation of Certified Shareholder Reports as Exchange Act Periodic Reporting Forms: Disclosure Required by Sections 406 and 407 of the Sarbanes-Oxley Act of 2002." Release No. 34-47262, 27 Jan. 2003.
14. "The Hot Seat: These Days, All Eyes are on the Chairman of the Audit Committee," *The Wall Street Journal*, 24 Feb. 2003, sec. R: 4.

auditors.[15] Obviously, when top executives perpetrate fraud, as Andrew Fastow, Enron's CFO allegedly did, the corporate governance processes have to be effectively and independently operating at the audit committee and board of directors' levels.

Facilitators of Corporate Governance

As we read in the previous section, the board of directors, audit committee, and executive management are primarily responsible for seeing that proper corporate governance is functioning within a public company; however, they cannot carry out all facets of corporate governance on their own. Even though the aforementioned parties actively carry out their administration responsibilities, four key facilitators are relied upon to properly execute and monitor effective corporate governance. These players include the **internal auditors**, the **external auditors**, **exchange markets** (including **financial analysts**), and **absentee owners**. Facilitators of corporate governance are indicated in Exhibit 1-1 in square boxes with rounded corners. A brief description of each party is provided below.

Internal Auditors.   Internal auditors provide the quality control for a company's financial systems. Within a public company, the internal auditors are responsible for making sure that internal controls exist and are operating correctly. They play a substantial role in monitoring and managing the company's operations, information systems, financial reporting, and fraud-related risks. In addition, the internal audit function verifies that governance structures and processes are effectively working within company guidelines and external regulations. Investigating fraud and other irregularities is another important function performed by internal auditors. The internal audit function, when carried out properly, can be a major asset to audit committees of the board of directors and to management in assuring the company's financial information is properly gathered and reported. Ideally, internal auditors report directly to the audit committee.

Acting as a governance facilitator for both management and the audit committee presents an interesting problem for internal auditors. On the one hand, internal auditors typically work closely with management. In fact, internal auditors need the support and cooperation of executive management to perform their duties effectively. On the other hand, internal

---

15. United States, *Sarbanes-Oxley Act of 2002*, Sec. 204.

auditors must represent the eyes and the ears of the audit committee in evaluating the day-to-day activities and control processes of the company. Thus, internal auditors must balance being a valued and trusted resource to management as well as a potential whistleblower if management does not act in the best interest of absentee owners. If internal auditors do not handle difficult issues with tact and professionalism, the internal audit function's effectiveness may be compromised as a result of a breakdown in communications and cooperation.[16]

Several weeks before SEC lawyers filed civil fraud charges against WorldCom in 2002, internal auditor Cynthia Cooper discovered that Scott Sullivan (CFO) had utilized questionable bookkeeping practices to improperly record expenses as long-term assets. As Cooper attempted to probe deeper, she was discouraged by management, particularly Sullivan, from pursuing the investigation further. Undeterred by the opposition, pressure, and threat of serious consequences, Cooper quietly worked with a small team to uncover a massive accounting fraud. Cooper immediately alerted Max Bobbitt (head of WorldCom's audit committee) that Sullivan had inappropriately recorded billions in expenses as assets over the previous five quarters. The misstatements uncovered by Cooper and her team were at the heart of WorldCom's $9 billion accounting fraud.[17]

Before the recent scandals and subsequent reforms, the internal audit function was voluntary for public companies. Even when companies had internal auditors, these services were often outsourced to the external auditor—as was the case at Enron, where Arthur Andersen served as both the internal and external auditor. The Sarbanes-Oxley Act prohibits the accounting firm that provides the external audit from performing the internal audit function for the same client.[18]

External Auditors.   Although the internal audit department helps ensure adherence to current standards and regulations, the SEC requires that all public companies have their financial statements audited by an

---

16. Sridhar Ramamoorti, "Internal Auditing: History, Evolution, and Prospects," *Research Opportunities in Internal Auditing*, ed. Andrew Bailey, et al. (Altamonte Springs: Institute of Internal Auditors Research Foundation, 2003), 1–23. Accessed 19 Feb. 2004.
<http://www.theiia.org/iia/index.cfm?doc_id=3993>
17. TSC Staff. "WorldCom Fraud Centered on Connection Costs." *TheStreet.Com,* 27 June 2002. Accessed 19 Feb. 2004
<http://www.thestreet.com/markets/marketfeatures/10029290.html>.
18. United States, *Sarbanes-Oxley Act of 2002,* Sec. 201.

independent, external audit firm. The external auditors can rely on the work of the internal audit function to the extent that the internal audit function is deemed objective and competent. The independence and objectivity of the external auditor helps provide assurance to investors that management has correctly prepared and created financial statements in accordance with current standards. As noted previously, external auditors are hired by and report directly to the audit committee.

For many years, public accounting firms reaped huge profits by performing non-audit services for their audit clients (e.g., systems consulting, bookkeeping, various management functions, etc.). In fact, the amount of revenue generated was so high that external audit firms were allegedly compelled to discount audit fees in order to attract increased client demand for the more lucrative non-audit services

The performance of non-audit services has been a controversial topic for many years. Doubtful about the ability of public accounting firms to maintain independence while carrying out such services for their audit clients, government regulators, such as Arthur Levitt, former SEC Chairman, had made several unsuccessful attempts before the Enron debacle to tighten independence restrictions. In the wake of the Enron scandal, the scope-of-services debate reemerged with vigor, eventually ending with the passage of the Sarbanes-Oxley Act of 2002. Section 201 of the Sarbanes-Oxley Act drew a clear line around a list of prohibited services, including information systems implementation and provision of internal auditing services for an audit client.[19] Specific authorization was given for external auditors to perform some non-audit services; however, the following safeguards were established to boost auditor independence: (1) audit committee pre-approval of audit and non-audit services, and (2) disclosure of company pre-approval policies and audit and non-audit service fees to investors.

To illustrate the importance of the public's perception regarding the independence of the external auditor, at the end of 2001 (before the Sarbanes-Oxley Act was passed), Disney Co. became concerned with the public's perception of the company's consulting arrangements with PricewaterhouseCoopers, its auditor. Stockholders were concerned that Disney was paying the independent auditor four to five times as much in consulting fees as it was for the financial statement audit (PwC received $8.7 million in audit fees and approximately $43 million for non-audit services

---

19. Ibid.

from Disney in 2001[20]). The magnitude of the consulting revenues made some investors question whether PwC could independently and skeptically review the company's books. As a result, Disney announced in January 2002 that it would not enter into new consulting contracts with its external auditor.[21]

Exchange Markets. To raise capital to fund operations and expansion, companies offer portions of corporate ownership (stock) in return for a monetary investment. Once financial statements are prepared and audited, a public company uses a forum created by public exchange markets (e.g., NYSE and National Association of Securities Dealers Automated Quotation, NASDAQ) to offer stock to the public. The exchange markets have always sought to protect the interests of investors to some degree by imposing standardized restrictions and guidelines on publicly traded companies.

As the Enron scandal and other large accounting frauds unfolded, stock prices plummeted and public confidence in the markets weakened. Investment slowed as investors started to question whether other publicly traded securities might be inflated based on management misrepresentation. In order to restore investor confidence in the public exchange markets, the exchanges imposed more stringent restrictions on listed companies.

In many instances, restrictions imposed by the New York Stock Exchange and National Association of Securities Dealers are more stringent than the requirements of the Sarbanes-Oxley Act. Two examples are the restrictions placed on audit committee members. First, the Sarbanes-Oxley Act requires that all audit committee members be independent unless specifically exempted by the SEC. The NYSE requires a minimum of three independent members on the audit committee and provides for no exceptions to its own rules. Second, the Sarbanes-Oxley Act does not address the issue of "cooling-off periods," which are used to prevent audit committee members from supervising the financial reporting processes they have influenced as former employees. Both NYSE and NASD rules prohibit service on the audit committee if members have been employed by the

---

20. David Lieberman, "Eisner: Disney Won't Use Auditor for Consulting," *USA Today,* 1 Jan. 2002. Accessed 19 Feb. 2004. <http://www.usatoday.com/money/earns/2002-01-31-disney.htm>.
21. Nanette Byrnes, et al. "Auditing Here, Consulting Over There." *BusinessWeek online* 8 Apr. 2002 Accessed 19 Feb. 2004 <http://www.businessweek.com/magazine/content/02_14/b3777051.htm>.

corporation or its auditors during the past five (NYSE) or three (NASD) years.[22]

Analysts. Securities analysts play an important role on Wall Street by examining the financial statements and other information relating to public companies, and by issuing earnings forecasts and stock recommendations (i.e., "buy," "hold," or "sell") for those companies. Analysts' persistent questioning even helped bring the Enron fraud to light. However, during the period of "irrational exuberance" (mid-1990s to 2000) many analysts allegedly issued overly optimistic stock recommendations and earnings forecasts to inflate stock prices and boost trading. By inflating prices and boosting trade volume, analysts and their firms reaped enormous financial rewards, with top analysts earning salaries and commissions in the tens of millions of dollars. One of the primary motives for inflating recommendations and earnings forecasts was to obtain (or retain) investment banking clients. Many research analysts work for companies that provide both investment banking and brokerage services. Investment bankers help companies raise money by selling securities to the general public (initial or secondary public offerings). Investment banks typically earn a percentage of the money raised from the sale of securities, which can be very substantial. Until recently, it was a common practice of investment bankers to involve brokerage research analysts in their business proposals. In this conflicted environment, analysts were allegedly pressured to issue optimistic recommendations and earnings forecasts to boost trade and to strengthen relationships with existing and potential investment banking clients. Unfortunately, the evidence supports the allegations. For example, at one point in 2001, only 29 of the 8,000 analyst stock recommendations issued to the public were "sell" recommendations.[23]

Subsequent litigation revealed that some analysts did, in fact, intentionally mislead the public. For example, well-known Internet analyst Henry Blodgett, who worked for Merrill Lynch, gave positive buy recommendations on stocks he privately referred to in internal

---

22. Robert Richardson and Charles Baril, "Can Your Audit Committee Withstand the Market's Scrutiny of Independence?" *SmartPros*, Feb. 2003. Accessed 19 Feb 2004
<http://smartpros.com/x36978.xml>.
23. "Wall Street—CBS Report," *NineMSN*, 11 Feb. 2001.
<http://businesssunday.ninemsn.com.au/businesssunday/Stories/default.asp>.

correspondence as "dogs" or "pieces of junk."[24] Mr. Blodgett has since been banned from the securities business and fined several million dollars. In 2003, evidence supporting allegations of misleading recommendations and earnings forecasts led the largest Wall Street firms to agree to a $1.4 billion global settlement with the SEC and the New York State Attorney. As part of the settlement, Wall Street firms agreed not to use brokerage analysts in connection with investment banking business.

In response to Section 501 of the Sarbanes-Oxley Act, in 2003 the SEC issued the rule titled, "Regulation Analyst Certification" (AC), which requires that brokers and dealers include in research reports certifications by the financial analyst that the views expressed in the report accurately reflect the analysts' personal views, and disclose whether or not the analyst received compensation or other payment in connection with the specific recommendations or views.

Regulation AC also makes threatening or retaliating against analysts issuing an unfavorable research report a criminal offense. Regulation AC is intended to promote the integrity of research reports and investor confidence in those reports. In 2002, the SEC also approved rule changes filed by the New York Stock Exchange and the National Association of Securities Dealers intended to mitigate analyst conflicts of interest.

Absentee Owners. Investors and creditors, who provide funding to public companies, are the absentee owners; they delegate all aspects of management of the companies, from strategic positioning to the daily business operations, to the executive management team. Even though the absentee owners may place considerable trust in the ability and integrity of management to run the enterprise, investors are ultimately responsible for obtaining, understanding, and analyzing the information they use as they make investment decisions.[25]

Today, investors and creditors demand great accountability from those on whom they depend for information. Some of the most powerful investors are "institutional investors" (e.g., Fidelity, Vanguard, and TIAA-CREF), who actively follow company performance and financial reporting. They ask tough questions, and are capable of exerting considerable influence on boards and management. One organization, known as *The*

---

24. "Wall Street Pays $1 Billion for Mistakes," *CNN* news transcripts 21 Dec. 2002. Accessed 20 Feb. 2004 <http://www.cnn.com/TRANSCRIPTS/0212/21/tt.00.html>.
25. S. A. DiPiazza Jr. and R. G. Eccles, *Building Public Trust*, 2002.

Council of Institutional Investors, has over 130 pension fund members whose assets exceed $2 trillion, and is recognized as a significant voice supporting the interests of institutional investors. For example, in May of 2003, this organization sent a letter to the SEC, and called on all U.S. shareholders to immediately contact the SEC, to support changes to the proxy rules and regulations that would give shareholders, especially substantial, long-term shareholders or groups of shareholders, more of a voice in selecting candidates for corporate boards.[26]

Regulators, Overseers, and Standard-Setters

As demonstrated in the previous section, proper facilitation of corporate governance requires participation and cooperation from a number of different parties. This section summarizes the role of the final participants in corporate governance: regulatory agencies, oversight boards, and standard-setters. Except for the SEC itself, these parties are indicated in triangles in Exhibit 1-1. These organizations help ensure fair, uniform participation, and cooperation of the various parties involved in carrying out corporate governance.

Securities and Exchange Commission (SEC).   As noted earlier, in 1934, the United States Congress delegated the authority and responsibility of overseeing and regulating all publicly traded companies and exchange markets to the **Securities and Exchange Commission**. The following chapters will focus primarily on the structure, legal framework, and operations of the SEC.

Because of the widespread nature of the oversight responsibilities carried by the Commission, the SEC incorporates the assistance of various other entities to meet its objectives.

Financial Accounting Standards Board (FASB).   In order to ensure uniform financial information for the public to use when making investment decisions, standardized reporting requirements are necessary. In 1973, the SEC appointed the FASB as the recognized standard-setter for the financial statements and disclosures to be filed with the SEC. The primary responsibility of the FASB is to create Generally Accepted Accounting Principles (GAAP), to which all public companies must adhere. The FASB is

---

26. "Shareholders Urged to Write SEC," Council of Institutional Investors, 22 May 2003. Accessed 20 Feb. 2004 <http://www.cii.org>

made up of members from the business, academic, and accounting professions; it is not a government entity. The FASB has no legal oversight or enforcement authority. In other words, the FASB does not issue fines, sanctions, or initiate legal action against non-compliers. However, both the American Institute of Certified Public Accountants (AICPA, discussed below) and the SEC recognizes the FASB as the official accounting standard-setting body for public companies. The AICPA requires auditors to comply with GAAP and the SEC has legal enforcement and sanction authority, thus these organizations lend the FASB the necessary authority to set accounting standards.

American Institute of Certified Public Accountants (AICPA). In the past, the AICPA, a private professional organization, played a major oversight role in corporate governance. As mandated by the SEC, all public companies are required to be audited by a firm of independent **Certified Public Accountants** (CPA). Prior to 2003, the AICPA set standards and regulations governing CPA firms that were permitted to conduct external audits of publicly traded companies. As part of the AICPA code of conduct, CPAs are required to ensure that public companies comply with GAAP. Until 2003, the AICPA's Auditing Standards Board established standards for how financial statement audits were to be conducted. These standards are known as Generally Accepted Auditing Standards (GAAS). As is the case with the FASB, the AICPA is not a government entity; however, it had been granted authority from the SEC to establish auditing standards. Following the accounting scandals of 2001 and 2002, many in Congress believed radical changes needed to take place in the regulation and oversight of the accounting profession. The AICPA was severely criticized for failing in its role in the self-regulation of the auditing profession. As a result of the Sarbanes-Oxley Act, and the establishment of the Public Companies Accounting Oversight Board (PCAOB, discussed below) the AICPA was forced to relinquish its oversight and regulatory authority for audits of public companies. Many of the responsibilities and operations once fulfilled by the AICPA have been reassigned to the PCAOB and other governmental bodies; however, the AICPA continues to issue auditing standards for non-public entities and to administer the examination required for the Certified Public Accountant designation.

Public Companies Accounting Oversight Board (PCAOB). As part of the reform mandated by the Sarbanes-Oxley Act, the SEC established an oversight board to take the place of the AICPA in overseeing, regulating, and disciplining CPA firms that conduct audits on publicly traded companies. As outlined in the Act, the board was created to "protect the interests of investors and further the public interest in the preparation of informative, accurate, and independent audit reports for companies."[27]

This new board, PCAOB, is a non-profit corporation funded by SEC registrants and public accounting firms. The board is made up of five members, appointed by the SEC, who must all be "financially literate." Of the five board members, only two can be, or have been, certified public accountants; the remaining three members cannot be, or have been, a CPA. The chairperson can only be a CPA if that person has not practiced for at least five years prior to his/her appointment to the board.

Under the Sarbanes-Oxley Act, all audit firms wishing to perform audits of public companies must register with the PCAOB and meet standards set by the board. Accordingly, the PCAOB received the authority and responsibility to register and inspect CPA firms that audit public companies, establish audit standards, enforce compliance with Sarbanes-Oxley and PCAOB rules, and investigate registered audit firms for potential violations.[28] Although the board is granted authority by the Sarbanes-Oxley Act, they fall under the jurisdiction and oversight of the SEC.

OVERVIEW AND SUMMARY

Companies seeking to raise external funding to further their operations and achieve corporate goals often turn to public securities exchange markets to offer shares of ownership (stock) or disaggregated loan amounts (bonds) to the general public. As members of the public invest their resources in a company by purchasing stocks or bonds, they become absentee owners of the company. The absentee owners are not involved in the daily operations of the company; they delegate stewardship over resources and the responsibility of running the company to management. Because of the "inside" position held by management, it has access to information regarding the financial condition and general operations of the company that are not accessible to the absentee owners. This information asymmetry, combined with greed and personal incentives, can lead management to improperly utilize invested resources or to withhold or inaccurately report

---

27. *Sarbanes-Oxley Act of 2002*, op. cit, Sec. 101.
28. United States, *Sarbanes-Oxley Act of 2002*, (2002): Sec. 101.

information for personal benefit. Incentives, opportunities, irrational investment practices, and the lack of effective corporate governance led to a rash of devastating scandals in the 1920s and again around the turn of the twenty-first century. At both these points in history, Congress passed landmark legislation to improve corporate governance.

As shown in Exhibit 1-2, corporate governance includes all aspects of a company's performance including appropriate accountability and stewardship over resources, risk management, operational and marketing strategies, internal control, conformance with applicable laws and regulations, public relations and communications, and financial reporting. However, corporate governance exists in order to protect the interests of the absentee owners and to ensure the proper utilization of invested resources and accurate information disclosure by executive management. In other words, the fundamental objective, or foundation, of corporate governance is to protect the interests of the absentee owners and other key stakeholders. Once this foundation is firmly established, the board of directors, the audit committee, and executive management are empowered to make responsible

Exhibit 1-2: Aspects of Corporate Governance

The figure was adapted from a similar figure in KPMG's, "Audit Committee Roundtable Highlights, Spring 2003: Building a Framework for Effective Audit Committee Oversight," © 2003 KPMG International, http://www.kpmg.com/aci.

strategic and operational decisions within a framework of sound corporate governance. As shown by past accounting scandals and securities frauds, adequate corporate governance is critical to the continued success and credibility of public companies and the U.S. financial system.

Fair and accurate financial reporting is a key goal of effective corporate governance. Financial reporting is a common criterion used internally and externally to measure the effective operation and oversight of a company's strategy, management, and resources. The fairness and accuracy of financial reporting is a key accountability mechanism by which the owners and other stakeholders (e.g., customers, vendors, regulators) evaluate parties responsible for corporate governance are held responsible for their actions.

The remainder of this text focuses on the top of the pyramid illustrated in Exhibit 1-2: financial reporting and the central role played by the SEC in ensuring the accuracy, adequacy and fairness of financial reporting to the marketplace.

DISCUSSION QUESTIONS

1. What corporate scandals led to the Sarbanes-Oxley Act of 2002? How were these events similar to those that led up to the Securities Acts of 1933 and 1934?

2. Explain why there is a need for effective corporate governance and whose interests are at stake. What role does "information asymmetry" play?

3. Name the parties primarily responsible for corporate governance and briefly summarize their primary roles and responsibilities.

4. Why are the qualities of objectivity and independence important in boards of directors and audit committees?

5. What parties play an important role as facilitators of corporate governance?

6. Why are auditors considered as facilitators rather than as one of the parties primarily responsible for corporate governance?

7. Summarize the role the SEC plays in promoting and overseeing effective corporate governance.

8. How has the role of the AICPA changed as a result of Sarbanes-Oxley? What were the reasons for this change, and what is the primary implication for the accounting profession?

9. How does fair financial reporting relate to corporate governance?

2

Origin and Nature of the SEC

The Securities and Exchange Commission (SEC) is an independent, bipartisan, quasi-judicial agency of the United States government. The SEC was established by the United States' Congress in 1934, in conjunction with the passage of the 1933 and 1934 Securities Acts, to help regulate the U.S. securities markets. Since that time, the SEC has played a very important role in the business community. This chapter describes in more detail the reasons for the establishment of the SEC, its organizational structure, and the nature of its current operations.

ORIGIN OF THE SEC

To provide a proper historical perspective, we will first discuss the history of commerce, the corporate form of business, the development of capital markets, and the need for disclosure of financial information.

Historical Background

In the early days of commerce barter was the primary means for conducting business transactions. Goods and services were traded directly for other goods and services. Businesses were conducted as proprietorships or sometimes as partnerships and joint ventures. Generally, the managers and the owners of business were the same individuals. External reporting of the results of operations by these closely held commercial entities was generally not necessary. Internal information for planning and control was needed however, and accounting systems were introduced to help provide that information. Although several forms of financial record keeping had been utilized for millennia, it was not until the Italian Renaissance that double entry accounting was popularized by Luca Pacioli.[1] The need for agreed-upon forms of accounting became more pressing as businesses began to seek outside investment. Outside investors needed a way to determine if business owners and managers were good stewards of the company's assets.

Establishment and Early Regulation of Capital Markets

As commercial enterprises multiplied both in size and number, more and more people were attracted to business opportunities, and the investment of capital resources expanded rapidly. The more aggressive businesses soon realized the financial advantage of encouraging capital investment by people who were willing to assume the risks of ownership, but in most cases were neither willing nor able to assist in management. An advantage of developing the corporate form of business was that ownership and financial interest could be spread over a broad base by issuing securities. Ownership and management thus became separated, and there was a need for a marketplace where stock and debt instruments could be exchanged for invested capital resources. This need led to the establishment of extensive capital markets first in Europe and then in the United States.

The corporate form of business also increased the need for objective verification of data and created a need for accurate and adequate information disclosure to owners and potential investors. As capital markets increased in size and activity, an irresponsible attitude developed in some corporate officers who took advantage of lax conditions in the securities markets and profited by distorting data and manipulating the markets. Governments, sensing some responsibility to protect those who invested in corporations, made faltering attempts to create a working partnership between management and investors and to ensure an adequate supply of capital available for sound economic growth.

For example, as early as 1285, King Edward I attempted to gain some control over burgeoning capital markets by authorizing the Court of

---

1. John Alexander, "History of Accounting," Association of Chartered Accountants in the United States. Accessed 3 Sep. 2003 <http://www.acaus.org/acc_his.html>.

Aldermen to license brokers located in London. In the early 18th century, France and England experienced a mania of speculative investment centered on the development of trading companies doing business in the Western Hemisphere. At one point, scheme offers exceeded £300 million sterling in the aggregate—more than the value of all the land in Great Britain.[2] Parliament was incensed over the abuses and retaliated with the harsh Bubble Act of 1720, holding issuers and brokers liable for damages and losses resulting from dishonest issues of securities.

Regulation of Securities in the United States

The pattern of securities legislation in the United States followed the example of Great Britain: with widespread abuses that were made obvious by a number of financial scandals and crisis. In response to scandal and crisis, the government launched a series of retrospective investigations to determine how the frauds were conducted and how they were able to go undetected. The government then passed restrictive laws to restore order and trust to the securities markets. Thus, as illustrated in Chapter 1, large portions of the U.S. securities laws have been built in response to widespread abuses and fraud. Given the nature of equity markets and the desire for wealth, it seems safe to assume there will more abuses and fraud in the future.

A popular misconception is that securities regulation in the United States resulted solely from the stock market crash in 1929 and the ensuing years of financial stagnation. However, the financial difficulties of the 1930s only provided the last straw. Long before the crash of 1929, there were movements to regulate the securities markets through federal laws.

Early Federal Attempts. Federal securities legislation had been sought since the late 19th century. In 1885, discussion surfaced concerning federal licensing of companies involved in interstate commerce. The Federal Trade Commission Act and the Clayton Act resulted from efforts to gain federal control during the first years of the 20th century. The Industrial Commission, established by Congress in 1898, reported in 1902 that public disclosure of material information of all publicly held corporations should be mandatory and should include annual financial reports. During the next two decades, three major bills seeking greater disclosure were introduced

---

2. Louis Loss, and Joel Seligman, *Securities Regulation,*. 3rd ed. (New York: Aspen Law & Business, 1998), 4.

into Congress but none was ever reported out of committee to either the House or the Senate. The time was not right; a serious financial plight was not present to spur such legislation.

State Regulation.   While the federal government was searching for its role in securities legislation, state governments were making some attempts to bring order to chaotic securities markets. Kansas led the way in 1911 to combat the bleeding of the "Agrarian West" by the "Moneyed East."[3] By 1913, 22 other states had passed laws aimed at regulating the sale of securities. Divided into two categories, these laws were: (1) fraud laws, which imposed penalties if evidence indicated fraud had been committed in the sale of securities; and (2) regulatory laws, which attempted to prohibit the sale of securities until an application was filed and permission was granted by the state.[4] These early laws became known as "blue-sky" laws after a judicial decision characterized some transactions as "speculative schemes which have no more basis than so many feet of 'blue sky'."[5]

State laws, for several reasons, never proved totally effective in regulating securities markets. Of primary consideration was the interstate nature of the U.S. economic system. The absence of legislation in some states and the inadequacy of laws in others allowed fraudulent and deceptive practices to continue in spite of regulatory efforts. A witness, cited in a study submitted by the Department of Commerce in 1933, indicated that "the most effective and widely used method of evading the provisions of State blue-sky laws consists in operating across state lines."[6]

The effectiveness of blue-sky laws was weakened by exemptions inserted by state legislatures as well as by lax enforcement by state officials. State legislatures seemed more concerned about having a law on the books than about enforcing proper regulation of securities sales.

Complicating state enforcement was nearly universal willingness of victims to condone the offense or to accept a compromise. If a state began

---

3. Ibid., p. 27.
4. Jacob Lasser, and J.A. Gerardi, *Federal Securities Act Procedure*, (New York: McGraw-Hill, 1934), 2.
5. Hall v. Geiger-Jones, 242 U.S. 539, 550 (1917).
6. U.S. Department of Commerce, "A Study of the Economic and Legal Aspects of the Proposed Federal Securities Act," reprinted in Federal Securities Act: Hearings before House Committee on Interstate and Foreign Commerce on H.R. 4314, 73rd Cong. 1st sess. (Washington, D.C.: Government Printing Office, 1933), 100.

preparing evidence against a corporation, the company would pay investors for a part of the loss, causing the state to lose its witness and the case.

Abuses during the 1920s. The securities market activities of the 1920s are legendary. While trading and investment were brisk, the underlying strength of the market was eroding as a result of certain common practices.[7] The first was price manipulation. It was somewhat common for brokers or dealers to indulge in "wash sales" or "matched orders," in which successive buy and sell orders created a false impression of activity and forced prices up. This maneuver allowed those involved to reap huge profits before the price fell back to its true market level. Outright deceit by issuing false and misleading statements was another improper practice. The objective of these manipulative acts was to make profits at the expense of unwary investors.

One classic example of a major securities fraud is the Ivar Kreuger case. During the 1920s, the most widely held securities in the United States, and perhaps the world, were the stocks and bonds of Kreugar & Toll, Inc., a Swedish match company. These securities were popular because they paid high dividends (over 20 percent annually) and were sold in small denominations, making them attractive to both large and small investors. Ivar Kreugar, known as the "Match King," became famous and wealthy as a financial genius, building his business into a multi-billion-dollar international enterprise. In fact, Kreugar defrauded millions of investors by personally creating false and misleading financial statements. Instead of being paid out of profits, the dividends were paid out of capital that was raised by selling new securities to unsuspecting investors. Eventually, in 1932, the giant pyramid collapsed, Kreugar committed suicide, and Kreugar & Toll, Inc. went bankrupt. On the day Kreugar died, his company's stock was selling for $5 a share. Within weeks, it was selling for five cents a share. The American public was outraged, and some have speculated that this major fraud was instrumental in causing Congress to enact securities legislation in hopes of preventing this from happening again.[8]

Another practice undermining securities markets was the excessive use of credit to finance speculative activities. This is commonly referred to as buying stocks "on margin." Margin requirements were only ten percent,

---

7. Securities and Exchange Commission 25th Annual Report Washington: Government Printing Office, 1960. XV-XVII. The Foreword to this report is obviously an attempt to support the SEC, but it does provide valuable information about the background of the SEC.
8. Dale Flesher, and Tonya Flesher, "Ivar Kreugar's Contribution to U.S. Financial Reporting," *The Accounting Review*, 61 (3) (1986): 421–434.

which meant investors could buy $10 in stock with only $1 of their own funds.[9] As a result, a slight decline in market prices could start a chain reaction that would gain momentum when overextended customers sold out because a margin could not be covered. Such a situation became critical when the market began to decline drastically late in 1929 and early in 1930.

The misuse of corporate information by corporate officials and other "insiders" was another practice that led to instability in the securities markets. When management or executive officers engage in insider trading, they use important private and unpublished information to make trades at a profit, or to "tip" others to buy or sell securities. Executive officers also manipulated the markets by timing the release of information to the public about corporate activities.

The public outcry arising from the great decline in stock prices between 1929 and 1933 motivated the passage of the major federal laws regulating the securities industry. During the late 1920s, investors speculated excessively. About 55 percent of all personal savings were used to purchase securities and the public was severely affected when the Dow-Jones Industrial Average fell 89 percent between 1929 and 1933.

During this period, security price manipulation was common and satisfactory information concerning securities usually was not available. Regulation was badly needed. It is fortunate that legislation passed during such a period of strong reaction against the industry seems to have been basically good legislation.[10]

Awakening to the Need.   As state laws proved ineffective, government officials became concerned that "a supplemental Federal law was needed to stop this gap through which were being wasted hundreds of millions of dollars of public savings that might otherwise have been diverted to substantial industrial development."[11] The aggregate value of all stocks listed on the New York Stock Exchange was $89 billion before the market declined in autumn of 1929. In September and October, the aggregate value dropped by $18 billion. After those two disastrous months, it appeared for a short time that a recovery was under way, but the market softened in the spring of 1930, and a bear market prevailed over the next two and a half years. In

9. Layth Matthews, "What Caused the Great Depression of the 1930s?" *Gold Ocean*. Accessed 5 Sep. 2003 <http://www.shambhala.org/business/goldocean/causdep.html>.

10. Edward Willet, *Fundamentals of Securities Markets*, (New York: Appleton-Century-Crofts, 1968), 211.

11. Lasser and Gerardi, op. cit. 4.

1932, the aggregate value of stocks was only $15 billion—83% lower than the value in 1929.

The transition from state to federal regulation came with contest, however, and a traumatic awakening to the need for federal legislation. As Loss points out, "Whether any legislation could prevent another such catastrophe is beside the point; it is a simple fact that the developments of 1929-1932 brought the long movement for federal securities regulation to a head."[12]

It is interesting to note that the passage of the Securities Acts, and additional legislation since, has not fully prevented other significant declines in the overall stock market. For example, on October 18, 1987, the Dow-Jones Industrial Average fell 508.32 points, a decline of 22.6 percent. This was far more than the 12.8 percent decline on October 28, 1929, which generally is considered the start of the Great Depression.[13] It is significant, however, that the capital markets were able to withstand the 1987 stock market crash without the economy being thrown into a decade-long depression. In fact, Gross Domestic Product (GDP) growth in the year after the 1987 decline was stronger than the GDP growth in the prior year. Some argued that the quicker rebound of 1987 was evidence of a strong and credible market due to federal regulation. However, the market decline and widespread scandals uncovered in the 2000–2003 timeframe provided evidence additional federal regulation was necessary.[14]

Federal Action.   In March 1932, the Senate passed a resolution allowing the Banking and Currency Committee to investigate the securities industry. The subsequent far-reaching investigation uncovered a variety of problems. A report to the House of Representatives highlighted the extent of losses incurred by the investing public due to the practices of issuers and brokers:

> During the post-war decade some 50 billions of new securities were floated in the United States. Fully half or $25,000,000,000 worth of securities floated during this period have been proved to be worthless. These cold figures spell tragedy in the lives of

---

12. Loss and Seligman, op. cit., 120-121.
13. Kenneth Bacon, "The Crash of '87 —Stocks Plunge 508.32 Amid Panicky Selling," *The Wall Street Journal,* 20 Oct. 1987, p. 1.
14. The S&P 500 and NASDAQ indices declined 45 and 69 percent, respectively, between January 2000 and March 2003.

thousands of individuals who invested their life savings, accumulated after years of effort, in these worthless securities. The flotation of such a mass of essentially fraudulent securities was made possible because of the complete abandonment by many underwriters and dealers in securities of those standards of fair, honest, and prudent dealing that should be basic to the encouragement of investment in any enterprise. Alluring promises of easy wealth were freely made with little or no attempt to bring to the investor's attention those facts essential to estimating the worth of any security. High-pressure salesmanship rather than careful counsel was the rule in this most dangerous of enterprises.[15]

Several philosophies abounded as Congress approached the task of legislation. Many advocated a fraud law patterned after New York's Martin Act because they saw preventive laws as unworkable and unenforceable hindrances to honest business. Those at the other extreme wanted laws patterned after the laws of several other states that required securities registration and strict qualification. A compromise group spoke for disclosure laws similar to the English Companies Act of 1900.[16]

Establishment of the SEC

With disclosure being a primary concern, Congress sought securities regulation that would blend the various philosophies. The results were the Securities Act of 1933 and the Securities Exchange Act of 1934. It was under the authority of the latter act that the Securities and Exchange Commission was created. The SEC was given the duty to ensure "full and fair" disclosure of all material facts concerning securities offered for public investment. The Commission's intent was not necessarily to prevent speculative securities from entering the market, but to insist that investors be provided with adequate information. In conjunction with the adequate disclosure objective, two additional, important objectives of the SEC are the initiation of litigation in cases of fraud and the provision for proper registration of securities.

---

15. The House Committee on Interstate and Foreign Commerce, Federal Supervision of Traffic in Investment Securities in Interstate Commerce, Report No. 85, 73d Cong. 1st sess. (Washington, D.C.: Government Printing Office, 1934), 2.
16. Loss and Seligman, op. cit., Chapter 1G.

In a 1975 interview, John C. Burton, then Chief Accountant for the SEC, provided the following justification for the SEC:

> In a broad sense we hope it [disclosure regulations] will contribute to a more efficient capital market . . . . The way in which we hope that will be achieved is first by giving investors more confidence that they are getting the whole story and second by encouraging the development of better tools of analysis and more responsibility on the part of the professional analyst to understand what's going on. We think that by giving them better data we can encourage them in the direction of doing a better job, thus leading, we hope, to more effective capital markets.[17]

Growth of the SEC.   The SEC has experienced an interesting maturation process. The infancy and adolescence of the Commission extended to 1945 and were characterized by the working out of kinks in legislation and the establishment of the administrative procedures necessary for the new agency. Early commissioners had to be salespeople as much as interpretative geniuses; they inspired confidence in the laws and at the same time enforced them. By 1945 the SEC began to reach maturity. Then, for approximately the next 15 years, the Commission concentrated on performing the function assigned by the laws as interpreted in previous years. Thus, this period was characterized by very little significant legislation or innovation; the post–World War II years were years marked by public confidence in the securities industry. The SEC's focus on implementation resulted in somewhat wider dissemination of information and greater disclosure.

A new round of legislative inquiry into the adequacy of existing securities legislation was initiated after a market break in May of 1962, which stopped three years of speculative frenzy in glamour stocks. A revitalization of the SEC followed, culminating in significant legislation with the 1964 Amendments to the Exchange Act. The 1960s also witnessed a growth of litigation related to the liabilities for the accuracy of registration statements, the provisions for which are contained in Section II of the 1933 Act. Because of the rapid increase in institutional investors through the 1960s, the SEC conducted a multi-year investigation on the effects of the trading of investment companies on the market. This investigation resulted in the 1970 amendments to the Investment Company Act of 1940. In 1977,

---

17. "An Interview with John C. Burton," *Management Accounting*, 56 (11) (1975): 19–23.

the Foreign Corrupt Practices Act was enacted to combat corporate bribery and illegal business practices. In 1984, the Insider Trading Sanctions Act became law, permitting the SEC to seek civil fines of up to three times illegal insider trading profits, gained by those who have been proven to have traded on the basis of material non-public information. In 1995, the Private Securities Litigation Reform Act was created to lessen the burden of liability of auditors in securities fraud litigations as well as to create new responsibilities for auditors to detect and report illegal activities. In 2000, the SEC adopted Regulation FD requiring issuing companies to make public disclosure of material non-public information shared with securities analysts and institutional investors. In 2002, Congress established a legislation landmark with the passage of the *Sarbanes-Oxley Public Company Accounting Reform and Investor Protection Act.* Among many other provisions, this Act tightened rules regarding auditor independence, corporate responsibility, and financial disclosure requirements.

The SEC and Accounting Standards.   Congressional investigations into the improper dealings of such companies as Enron, WorldCom, and Tyco, continue to raise questions concerning the structure of the capital markets and the effectiveness of the SEC and the accounting profession. One remarkable result of Sarbanes-Oxley was the requirement for the SEC to form a new organization to oversee audits of public companies—the Public Company Accounting Oversight Board (PCAOB). In 2003, the PCAOB assumed the regulatory and oversight roles previously held by the AICPA. This significant change, resulting in the loss of self-regulation for accountants, is one of many reforms that took place in the wake of the accounting scandals of 2001 and 2002. Of particular importance to accountants today are the questions being raised concerning the SEC's delegation of accounting rule making to the Financial Accounting Standards Board (FASB). The relationship of the SEC to the FASB is both unique and important. The 1933 Securities Act empowers the SEC with the authority to prescribe accounting standards to be followed by companies in complying with the federal securities laws.[18] Historically, however, the SEC has allowed private sector standard setting bodies to establish generally accepted accounting principles (GAAP). As discussed in Chapter 1, the FASB is the current accounting standard-setting body in the United States. The SEC

---

18. Sections 7, 19(a), and Schedule A of information required in registration, Schedule A (25) and (26) of the Securities Act of 1933.

endorsed the establishment of the FASB in 1973, and in 2003 reaffirmed the status of the FASB as the recognized private-sector standard setting body in SEC Policy Statement 33-8221, which begins as follows:

> The Securities and Exchange Commission has determined that the Financial Accounting Standards Board (FASB or Board) and its parent organization, the Financial Accounting Foundation (FAF), satisfy the criteria in section 108 of the Sarbanes-Oxley Act of 2002 and, accordingly, FASB's financial accounting and reporting standards are recognized as "generally accepted" for purposes of the federal securities laws.[19]

While the SEC has delegated a certain part of its responsibility for accounting standard setting to the FASB, the SEC continues to exercise strong oversight in the standard-setting process. The following excerpts from a speech of Robert Herdman, the Chief Accountant of the SEC in 2001 and 2002, show how the SEC views its relationship with the FASB:

> Practically since its inception, the Commission has looked to the private sector for leadership in establishing and improving the accounting methods used to prepare financial statements. The body currently performing that function is the Financial Accounting Standards Board, or the FASB. As a result, the FASB has the power to set, but not enforce, accounting standards to be used by public companies.
>
> In light of the SEC's unique role, it is critical that the SEC work closely with the FASB, particularly as it relates to the FASB's agenda. In addition, the SEC has the ultimate responsibility to ensure that the FASB deals with issues referred to it by the SEC. The cooperative effort between the public and private sectors has given the United States the best financial reporting system in the world, and the Commission is intent on making it even better.[20]

---

19. United States, Securities and Exchange Commission, "Reaffirming the Status of the FASB as a Designated Private-Sector Standard Setter," Policy Statement 33-8221, 25 Apr. 2003.
20. Robert Herdman, "Testimony Concerning the Roles of the SEC and the FASB in Establishing GAAP," Before the House Subcommittee on Capital Markets, Insurance, and Government Sponsored Enterprises, Cmte. on Financial Services. 14 May 2002. Accessed 21 Feb. 2004 <http://www.sec.gov/news/testimony/051402tsrkh.htm>.

In fulfilling its responsibility, the SEC on occasion has found it necessary to establish standards or to supplement or amend existing standards. Overall, however, the SEC consistently has concluded that the FASB is performing its tasks well.[21]

ORGANIZATIONAL STRUCTURE OF THE SEC

The SEC is directed by five commissioners, not more than three of whom may be of the same political party. The president of the United States with the advice and consent of the Senate appoints members of the Commission. Each commissioner is appointed for a five-year term with one member's term expiring each year. The president designates one member to chair the Commission.

The SEC is administered from its Washington, D.C. headquarters and has regional and branch offices in major financial centers of the United States. The organizational structure is illustrated by Exhibit 2-1. The commissioners are assisted by a staff of professionals, including accountants, engineers, examiners, lawyers, and securities analysts. These professionals are assigned to the various divisions and offices, including the regional offices, as shown in the organization chart.

SEC Divisions

There are four divisions at the SEC, some of which have overlapping authority. Cooperation among divisions is essential if the SEC is to function smoothly. The accounting practitioner and the business executive must be aware of the division of functions in order to comply successfully with securities statutes. Compliance with one division's requirements does not automatically ensure adherence to another division's rules.

---

21. Ibid.

Exhibit 2-1: Organizational Structure of the SEC

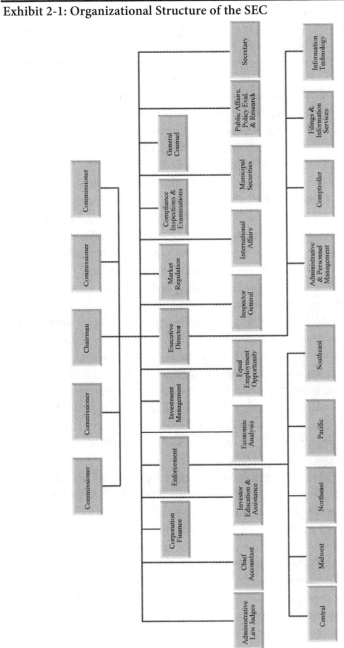

SOURCE: http://www.sec.gov/images/secorg.gif accessed 5 Sep. 2003.

Division of Corporation Finance. The Division of Corporation Finance is perhaps the most important division for individuals in business and specifically for legal, finance, and accounting professionals associated with financial reporting. The division's major responsibilities include: assisting the Commission in establishing and requiring adherence to standards of economic and financial reporting and disclosure by all companies under SEC jurisdiction; setting standards for the disclosure requirements of proxy solicitations; and administering disclosure requirements primarily for the Securities Act of 1933, the Securities Exchange Act of 1934, the Trust Indenture Act of 1939, and the Sarbanes-Oxley Act of 2002.

The Division of Corporation Finance reviews selected registration statements (lengthy and often complicated narrations of corporate operations), prospectuses, quarterly and annual reports, proxy statements, and sales literature. As we discuss these reports and filings later in the book, the reader will better understand just how significant the influence of this division is. Investigations, examinations, formal hearings, and informal conferences are used in the analysis and review of the myriad of reports handled each year by this division.

In addition to its review function, the Division of Corporation Finance also provides a useful interpretative and advisory service to help clarify to issuers, accountants, lawyers, and underwriters the application and requirements of the securities laws it administers. Since substantially all the financial statements submitted for review must be certified by independent accountants, a significant portion of an accountant's work with the SEC will be reviewed by this division. The advisory service has proved effective in avoiding problems by providing instructive guidance concerning registration and reporting procedures.

The Division of Corporation Finance is organized along industry lines. According to the SEC, this structure allows the division to better ascertain the particular disclosure needs of different industries and to more readily identify industry trends.

Division of Market Regulation. The Division of Market Regulation assists the Commission in the regulation of national securities exchanges and of brokers and dealers registered under the Investment Advisers Act of 1940. This Division cooperates with the regional offices of the SEC in investigating and inspecting exchanges, brokers, and dealers. This Division monitors trading markets, both exchanges and over-the-counter markets, and broker-dealers mainly through supervising the work of self-regulated organizations, such as the National Association of Securities Dealers (NASD). The objective of the surveillance is twofold. First, the division attempts to discourage manipulation or fraud in connection with the sale or purchase of securities. Second, the Division supervises the issuance of new securities and ensures adherence to rules regarding the stabilization of securities prices. Because the Commission has the power to suspend an exchange for up to one year, the activities of this Division are important and powerful.

The Division of Market Regulation also supervises the broker–dealer inspection program. Brokers and dealers are required to register with the SEC and are subject to periodic inspections of their activities. The periodic reports submitted by brokers/dealers are analyzed by this division to ensure proper disclosure and to foster the proper conduct of these dealers. The Commission is capable of exerting considerable control over the activities of brokers and dealers. It can, and does, permanently prohibit brokers/dealers from transacting business or, as is more often the case, suspend them for a shorter period of time. Not only does the Division supervise the markets, it also provides to investors and registrants interpretative advice on the requirements to the statutes it administers. This advisement service has proved effective in avoiding possible problems, and in reducing the division's subsequent workload.

An example of an action of this Division that affects both the trading markets and brokers/dealers is the adoption of two rules (11Ac1-5 and 11Ac1-6) on November 11, 2000. These rules require the various types of trading markets to report monthly their order execution quality on a stock by stock basis and brokers to report quarterly on which trading markets they route the majority of their orders through. These rules are efforts by the Division to promote market efficiencies and competition through providing more information to the investor-consumer regarding the quality of trade execution.

Division of Enforcement. The Division of Enforcement is responsible for reviewing and directing all enforcement activities of the regional offices, supervising investigations conducted pursuant to federal securities laws, and initiating injunctive actions. The Division must determine whether available evidence adequately supports allegations in complaints. Since it is responsible for reviewing cases sent to the Department of Justice for criminal prosecution, this division maintains close cooperation with the Office of the General Counsel.

Division of Investment Management. The Division of Investment Management assists the Commission in the administration of the Investment Company Act, the Investment Advisers Act, and in the execution of the Public Utility Holding Company Act. All investigations and inspections arising from these Acts and matters concerning the services provided by investment companies and dealers are the responsibilities of this Division. Reporting and enforcement requirements, however, are the responsibilities of other Divisions.

Major Offices

Several principal offices function under the Commission. The numerous regional and branch offices serve as field representatives for the administration and enforcement of federal securities legislation. These offices serve as the eyes and ears of the Commission and have the authority to initiate investigations into possible violations of securities laws, while working in connection with the divisions, the General Counsel, and the Chief Accountant. The *Federal Securities Law Reports* lists the following specific functions of regional offices:

- Investigate transactions in securities.
- Examine members of exchanges, broker-dealers, transfer agents, investment advisors, and investment companies.
- Prosecute injunctive actions.
- Render assistance to U.S. attorneys in criminal cases.
- Participate in cases under Chapters 9 and 11 of the Bankruptcy Code in specified geographic areas.
- Make the Commission's facilities more readily available to the general public of that region.

In addition to the above duties, the regional and branch offices serve the public in advisory roles concerning the different Acts.[22]

22. Federal Securities Law Reports, (Chicago: Commerce Clearing House, Inc.). ¶301-¶355 on Vol. 1 gives an excellent description of the organizations of the SEC, listing all divisions and offices. Andrew Downey Orrick has given a thorough report of divisional responsibilities in "Organization, Procedures and Practices of the Securities and Exchanges Commission," *The*

A major part of the investigative activities conducted by regional offices is concerned with brokers and dealers. All registered dealers are subject to surprise inspections to ensure compliance with statutory provisions related especially to accounting procedures; thus, accountants performing services for brokers or dealers should be fully aware of related statutory provisions.

Office of the Chief Accountant. Perhaps the most powerful accounting position in the United States is that of Chief Accountant of the SEC. The Office of the Chief Accountant is responsible to the Commission for all accounting and auditing matters that arise in the administration of the securities laws. A potentially confusing point is that each of the divisions of the SEC has a chief accountant. Those divisional chief accountant positions are separate and distinct from the Office of the Chief Accountant of the SEC.

As noted earlier, the SEC has been given statutory power to develop accounting principles. Thus, one of the primary responsibilities of the Chief Accountant is to work closely with the FASB, the PCAOB, and other interested parties in determining appropriate accounting and auditing standards and disclosure requirements. In addition, the Chief Accountant advises the Commission on the form and content of financial statements and other financial disclosures that are filed with the SEC, and supervises the procedures to be followed in auditing or accounting investigations conducted by the Commission staff. In this capacity there is extensive interaction between the Office of the Chief Accountant and SEC registrants and their auditors.

Not only does the Office of the Chief Accountant work closely with standard-setting bodies, registrants, and CPAs with SEC clients, it also serves as a consultant to the Division of Corporation Finance and the other divisions and offices of the SEC in all accounting and auditing matters. The Chief Accountant's staff is relatively small (approximately 60 professionals), but has significant experience and expertise, which is needed to handle their broad range of responsibilities. The oversight activities of this office are both significant and far-reaching in terms of their impact on the accounting profession.

George Washington Law Review, Vol. 28, No. 1 (October 1959), pp. 50–85. The organization has changed somewhat since Orrick's article, but it still serves as an excellent source.

Office of the General Counsel.   This office serves as the focal point for all appellate and other litigation brought by the Commission. The duties of this office include representing the Commission in judicial proceedings; handling multi-divisional legal matters; providing legal advice and assistance to the Commission, its divisions, and its offices with respect to statutory interpretation, rule making, legislative matters, and other legal issues. In addition, General Counsel supervises the SEC's responsibilities under the Bankruptcy Code.[23]

In the execution of these responsibilities, General Counsel can act on its own initiative as well as at the request of the Commission. The office helps prepare reports to Congress and coordinates the preparation of any legislative proposals offered by the Commission. The Office of General Counsel also reviews all cases in which criminal prosecution is recommended.

Other Offices.   Other offices provide vital support for SEC activities, but their work exceeds the scope of this book. The interested reader can find descriptive material in SEC publications.

SUMMARY

A popular misconception is that the U.S. federal securities laws that established the SEC resulted from the market crash of 1929 and the ensuing depression. It is true that these events triggered federal laws, but there had been attempts in the late 1800s to establish federal control and supervision of securities markets. The events of 2001–2003 provide a more recent illustration of financial scandals providing impetus to existing efforts to further legislate effective corporate governance practices.

Since public financing is an integral part of the U.S. economy, investor confidence in securities is imperative. When confidence was shaken during the Depression, restoration of public confidence was a major goal of public policy. The Securities Act of 1933 and the Securities Exchange Act of 1934, along with other statutes, were enacted to infuse a new spirit of trust in securities markets through protecting the public from losses from fraudulent or misrepresented securities. Disclosure of pertinent

23. United States. Securities and Exchange Commission. The Work of the SEC. Washington: The Office of Public Affairs, 1988. 36.

information, coupled with enforcement of the securities law, became the primary objectives of the newly created SEC. The role and responsibilities of the SEC were further expanded by subsequent legislation, especially the Sarbanes-Oxley Act of 2002.

To enable the SEC to accomplish its purposes, a network of operating divisions and offices, including regional offices, has been established. The divisions are organized along functional or industry lines with each division having responsibilities under one or more of the Securities Acts. Several staff offices lend specific, professional expertise to each of the operating divisions. Regional and branch offices are involved in the investigative activities of the Commission, but they also provide an effective network for receiving and disseminating important information.

A closer look at the laws administered by the SEC comprises the next chapter.

DISCUSSION QUESTIONS

1. How did businesses evolve into a state where external disclosure of financial information became necessary?

2. Was securities legislation in the 1930s the first attempt at regulation of capital markets? Explain.

3. What are the blue-sky laws? Explain the major categories of these laws. Have they been effective in regulating securities? Why or why not?

4. List the practices during the 1920s that led to the erosion of the stock market. Explain why those practices had such a negative effect.

5. What is the primary function of the SEC? Explain.

6. Some individuals view the establishment of the SEC as unnecessary and unproductive. Do you agree or disagree? Why?

7. What degree of influence does the SEC have in the securities markets? How do you see the SEC's role changing in relation to the securities markets during the next decade?

8. Describe the general characteristics of the organization of the SEC. Identify each of the divisions and explain the major purpose and function of each.

9. Explain the relationship between the SEC and the FASB.

10. What is the role of the Chief Accountant? Why is the role so significant for the accounting profession?

3

Legal Framework of the SEC

The SEC functions with the authority of law; in this chapter we focus on the Congressional Acts constituting the legal basis for the SEC. The actual Acts are long and detailed, so we only provide an introduction and overview. However, we do examine and explain the most relevant portions of each Act in sufficient detail so that the reader has a strong working knowledge of the SEC legal foundation and mandate. Readers interested in more comprehensive coverage should consider studying the Acts themselves and the additional references provided at the end of the book. The Acts are available on the SEC's Web site, http://www.sec.gov (in Chapter 5 we provide guidance on how to use and search the SEC's Web site).

Business executives and accountants must understand the fundamental concepts underlying the Acts establishing the SEC's legal framework, because several of the Acts outline executives' and accountants' roles and responsibilities, both statutory and assumed. These roles and responsibilities have evolved and expanded over the years as securities markets and financial reporting have increased in complexity and as the government and SEC have taken measures to increase public trust after corporate scandals. As a recent example, in reaction to the business and accounting scandals in 2002, executives of publicly traded companies must now personally certify that their companies' internal controls are effective and financial reporting fair. Likewise, beginning in 2004, management must hire public accountants to provide a certification (or opinion) regarding management's assertions as to the effectiveness of their companies' systems of internal control. (Independent accountants have, of course, been required to certify financial statements for their public-company clients since the 1933 and 1934 Acts, discussed below). With the increased complexity in financial reporting and the proliferation of different types of securities available in the marketplace, the shared role between accountant and business executive is vital to the credibility and success of the securities markets.

In addition to understanding the Acts, it is also important that business executives and accountants understand the ever-changing filing and reporting requirements promulgated by the SEC itself. Chapter 4 provides an overview of the process companies must follow to register with the SEC in order to sell their securities in the marketplace. Just as business professionals need to have a working knowledge of the Acts and be aware of changes in SEC requirements, it is likewise important for college students interested in careers in business to study these Acts and related requirements.

PURPOSE OF THE SEC

The stated purpose of the SEC is to ensure that securities investors receive "full and fair" information. The intent of Congress in establishing the SEC is summarized in the following SEC statement:

> Congress, in enacting the federal securities laws, created a continuous disclosure system designed to protect investors and to assure the maintenance of fair and honest securities markets. The Commission, in administering and implementing these laws, has sought to coordinate and integrate this disclosure system . . .

> The legislative history of the Securities Act of 1933 indicates that the main concern of Congress was to provide full and fair disclosure in connection with the offer and sale of securities.[1]

---

1. United States, Securities and Exchange Commission, "Notice of Adoption of Rule 146 under the Securities Act of 1933—'Transactions by Issuer Deemed Not to Involve Any Public

The expansive scope of the SEC's power and responsibility will become apparent as we outline the Acts in this chapter.

PRINCIPAL ACTS

Three principal Acts defining the SEC's mandate and legal framework are the Securities Act of 1933, the Securities Exchange Act of 1934, and the Sarbanes-Oxley Act of 2002. Both the 1933 and 1934 Acts have subsequently been revised and updated through amendments. For the most part, the financial reporting activities related to the SEC are controlled by these three Acts and by the specific forms, rules and disclosures required by the SEC in order to execute these Acts.

Securities Act of 1933

The first of the securities laws passed under Roosevelt's "New Deal" era was the Securities Act of 1933. This Act was designed to protect investors from false claims such as those that had existed prior to the stock market crash in 1929. The purpose of the 1933 Act is to regulate the initial offering and sale of securities through the mail system (interstate commerce). The 1933 Act does not concern itself with the trading of securities after their initial offering and sale by the issuing public company.

Objectives of the 1933 Act. The Securities Act of 1933, often referred to as the "truth in securities" law, has two basic objectives:

- To ensure investors are provided with all material information concerning securities offered for public sale; and
- To prevent misrepresentation, deceit, and other fraud in the sale of securities.[2]

The first objective is accomplished by requiring any firm offering securities for public sale, except those specifically exempted, to file a registration statement with the SEC and to provide potential investors with a prospectus that contains most of the information provided to the SEC.

Offering,'" Securities Act of 1933 Release No. 5487 23 Apr. 1974. SEC Docket 4 (5) 7 May 7, 1974, p. 155.

2. United States, Securities and Exchange Commission, *The Work of the SEC* (Washington, D.C.: The Office of Public Affairs, 1988), 7.

The law assumes that the disclosure of information concerning securities offerings will allow an investor to make a relatively informed choice among alternative investments.

With respect to the second objective, Sections 11 and 12 of the 1933 Act detail specific anti-fraud provisions. Section 11 outlines civil liability for submitting a false registration statement. Section 12 establishes civil liability for misleading investors through false statements, or not providing crucial information, in a prospectus or any communication, whether or not the security is required to be registered with the SEC. These fraud provisions enable investors to seek recompense from companies that omit important information or provide misleading information.

The stringent registration requirements of the 1933 Act do not prohibit speculative securities from entering the market, nor do they guarantee against losses. If the required information is provided in proper form, the SEC cannot prohibit the sale of securities, even though analysis may show the securities to be of questionable value. The investor, not the SEC, must ultimately judge the worth of the investment. However, the required disclosures are intended to provide the investor with the information necessary to make informed investment decisions.

While it is not the intent of the 1933 Act for the SEC to judge the merits of securities offered for sale, the SEC does, through its strict disclosure and reporting requirements, determine if the registration statement and the prospectus are deficient in their disclosure of required information. (The type and extent of SEC reviews are explained in more detail in Chapter 4.) The intent of the law is that "the Government should not take the responsibility for determining the investor's choice among investment opportunities but should make certain that the investor has an opportunity to make such choice on the basis of full disclosure of the pertinent facts and in the absence of fraud."[3] Thus, the 1933 Act is a "disclosure" statute. Disclosures are provided by means of a registration statement and a prospectus, both containing relevant financial and other information.

Obviously, the registration process itself does not guarantee the accuracy of the registration statement or the prospectus. However, severe penalties for false or misleading information certainly do discourage

3. United States, Cong. Senate. Committee on the Judiciary, *Economic Concentration - Part 8: Hearings on S. Res. 40 Before the Subcommittee on Antitrust and Monopoly of the Senate Committee on the Judiciary,* Hearing, 1970. 71st Cong., 2nd sess. p. 4834. (Statement of the Honorable Hamer H. Budge. At the time, Budge was the Chairman of the SEC.)

registrants from intentionally issuing false or misleading information. The 1933 Act provides investors the right to recover, through legal action, losses incurred as a result of false or misleading registrations and prospectuses. Section 11 of the 1933 Act states that anyone connected with the registration statement, including accountants, can be held liable for the accuracy of the statements. For example, Arthur Andersen, Enron's former auditor, faced numerous lawsuits brought by investors under the 1993 and 1994 Acts. (Chapter 6 discusses the liability of managers and accountants under the various Acts.)

Not all securities listed for sale must be registered with the SEC. The 1933 Act provides for certain exemptions, namely:

(1) Private offerings to a limited number of persons or institutions who have access to the kind of information that registration would disclose and who do not propose to redistribute the securities; (2) Offerings restricted to residents of the state in which the issuing company is organized and doing business; (3) Securities of municipal, state, federal and other governmental instrumentalities as well as charitable institutions, banks, and carriers subject to the Interstate Commerce Act; (4) Offerings not exceeding certain specified amounts made in compliance with regulations of the Commission; and (5) Offerings of "small business investment companies" made in accordance with rules and regulations of the Commission.[4]

The above exemptions may be divided into two main categories: (1) exempt securities, and (2) exempt transactions. Examples of securities that are exempt are those offered by banks, nonprofit organizations, governments, and common carriers. Also exempt are intrastate offerings of securities. An example of an exempt transaction is the sale of certain promissory notes secured by real estate.[5] It should be noted that these are exemptions from the registration requirements; these securities are still subject to the Act's prohibition of the use of interstate commerce to defraud.[6]

---

4. *The Work of the SEC, op.cit.*, 9–10.
5. For additional detail, see Section 3 and Section 4 of the Securities Act of 1933.
6. United States. *Securities Act of 1933*. Sec.17.

In addition to the examples of exemptions mentioned, the SEC has the authority under Section 3(b) of the 1933 Act to exempt other offerings when the amount of capital to be raised is small and the public offering is limited. Over the years, Congress and the SEC have approved an increase from $500,000 to $5,000,000 as the maximum amount that can be raised in a public offering without registration. Exemptions in this category must still comply with certain rules and regulations of the SEC. The Regulation A offering, under the 1933 Act, is the most common example of this type and is referred to as a "small issue exemption."

Although exempt from registration, Regulation A offerings require the use of an offering circular, similar to a prospectus, which contains financial and other information. The notification of the SEC and the filing of information also are required. Therefore, the procedures are very similar to registration, but the disclosure requirements are less extensive. The filings are received and reviewed by SEC regional offices in a manner similar to that used by the SEC's main office in Washington, D.C. for regular registration statements. Comments generally are received from the regional SEC offices, and notice of "no further comments" from a regional office indicates that the Regulation A offering may become effective.

Effect of 1933 Act on Accountants. Among the most important information contained in a registration statement and prospectus are the financial statements and supporting schedules, which must be certified by an independent public accountant (i.e., independent auditor). The certification must be a manually signed document accompanying the registration statement. The preparation and auditing of these financial reports in the manner required by the SEC is vitally important, and is the principal work done by internal company accountants and external auditors, respectively, under the 1933 Act.

Other work incidental to, but not required by, the 1933 Act includes the issuance of a "comfort letter" by an independent accountant to the underwriter. The underwriter, usually an investment bank, assumes the risk of buying a new issuance of a security and reselling it to the public, and thus acts as an intermediary between the issuer of the new security and the investing public. The underwriter of an issue has an obligation to exercise "due diligence" to verify the accuracy of the registration statement itself as well as any unaudited interim statements included to update the certified statements. The comfort letter from the company's independent accountant to the underwriter and legal counsel gives limited "negative assurance" on the unaudited financial statements of the issuer. Negative assurance means that the reviewing accountant has found no indication that the statements are false or misleading, but does not go so far as to express a *positive* opinion that the financial statements are, in fact, fairly stated. The accountant generally does not perform an audit of the interim statements but does perform a limited review of the statements and supporting information. The comfort letter is not a requirement of the 1933 Act and is not filed with the SEC, but generally it is requested by the underwriter as evidence that due diligence has been exercised concerning the reliability of the prospectus.[7]

Comfort letters generally are furnished pursuant to an underwriter's agreement and refer to one or more of the following subjects: (1) the independence of the accountants; (2) a statement of compliance as to form in all material respects of the audited financial statements and schedules required by the registration of securities under the Securities Act; (3) reference to the unaudited statements and their reasonableness; and (4) reference to significant changes in financial items since the date of the audited statements. Accountants also may be asked to comment on tables, statistics, and other financial information in the registration statement but should be careful not to go beyond their areas of expertise in giving comfort. Generally, the comfort letter will conclude with an explicit statement indicating that the letter is for use solely by the underwriters and is not to be filed as a part of the registration statement.

The accountant also performs the important function of providing assistance in reviewing, and submitting the financial statements and supporting schedules required in a registration statement. This function is discussed in more detail in Chapter 4.

Securities Exchange Act of 1934

Soon after passing the Securities Act of 1933, Congress moved to regulate the trading of securities in secondary markets through brokers and exchanges and to eliminate certain abuses in securities trading subsequent to their initial distribution. Congress also realized the necessity of having an

---

7. American Institute of Certified Public Accountants, "Letters for Underwriters and Certain Other Requesting Parties," Statement on Auditing Standards No. 72, *AICPA Professional Standards,* June 1, 2003 (Chicago: Commerce Clearing House, 2003). This statement explains the comfort letter and provides guidelines regarding its use, form, and application. See also "Interim Financial Information," Statement on Auditing Standards No. 71.

organization specifically authorized to carry out the functions outlined in the securities laws just passed. Thus, it was with passage of the Securities Exchange Act of 1934 that the SEC came into existence.

In general, the 1934 Act established the SEC's authority to regulate securities trading on the national exchanges. Unlike the 1933 Act, which restricts itself primarily to initial offerings, the 1934 Act is concerned with several aspects of securities trading. The 1934 Act initially extended the full and fair disclosure doctrine to include all companies that had securities registered on the national securities exchanges. In 1964, the Securities Acts Amendments extended the disclosure requirement to the securities of companies that trade on over-the-counter markets as well. This requirement is limited, however, to companies having over $10 million in total assets and 500 or more stockholders. In addition to other provisions to regulate the trading of previously issued securities across state boundaries, the 1934 Act provides for the registration of securities issuers, the registration of exchanges and brokers, and the protection of investors' interests.

Registration of Securities Issuers. Section 12 (a) of the Securities Exchange Act of 1934 states that companies desiring to have their securities traded on any of the national exchanges must file a registration statement quite similar to, although not as extensive as, the one required by the 1933 Act. This registration requirement is now extended to include over-the-counter-markets, except for the securities of small companies under the size limitations mentioned earlier. It must be understood that the 1933 and 1934 Acts are independent of each other, and registration under one Act does not necessarily meet the requirements of the other. The 1934 Act A does not require a prospectus because trading in secondary markets is open to everyone, and companies cannot determine who might be interested in their securities, and thus to whom they should provide a prospectus.

In addition to the registration of outstanding securities and the disclosures involved in that process, the 1934 Act requires that updated information be filed regularly with the SEC by means of periodic reports. The annual report to the SEC (Form 10-K) and the quarterly reports (Form 10-Q) are the most widely known and used periodic reports. (The most common SEC reports are described and illustrated in Chapter 5.) All information contained in these reports, with certain limited exceptions, is public information and is available at the offices of the SEC and on the SEC's Web site (http://www.sec.gov). While it is difficult to precisely measure the important benefits of the 1934 Act disclosures, for most major U.S. companies the costs and time involved in complying with the periodic reporting requirement of the 1934 Act are clearly significant.

As in the case of the 1933 Act, registration and continuous reporting do not guarantee accuracy. However, the SEC can file legal suits against those who prepare and file (or are associated with the filing of) fraudulent reports and can suspend the trading in securities of companies that fail to submit full and accurate reports or repeatedly fail to file on a timely basis.

Registration of Exchanges and Brokers.   Another important aspect of the 1934 Act is that it requires national securities exchanges to be registered. In its application for registration, a national exchange must file with the SEC a report giving comprehensive data concerning the rules of the exchange and the scope of its operations. The exchange also must agree to comply with the requirements of the 1934 Act and to enforce compliance by the brokers who are members of the exchange. The application will be approved if the SEC believes the exchange is organized in a manner that will allow it to adhere to the requirements of the law. The disclosures subsequently required of exchanges allow the SEC to monitor their activities.

Brokers dealing in over-the-counter markets also are required to register with the SEC. (Brokers who deal only in intrastate sales are exempt from this registration requirement.) The SEC has specified that registered brokers and dealers must submit periodic reports and records of transactions, and it has established minimum capital requirements for brokers. An extensive revision of these requirements was made in the SEC's Accounting Series Release (ASR) No. 156, dated April 26, 1974, and was incorporated into the SEC's Codification of Financial Reporting Policies in Financial Reporting Release (FRR) No. 1. This release specifies the ledgers, accounts, and journals that must be kept and such items as the maximum number of days that can elapse between any transaction and the posting or recording of that transaction.

Protection of Investors.   The 1934 Act contains other measures designed to provide fair securities markets for the investor. The Act forbids anyone from utilizing the interstate mails or national securities exchanges for any "manipulative or deceptive device or contrivance" designed to violate the rules and regulations established by the SEC. [Section 10(b)]. The 1934 Act specifically forbids such practices as wash sales and matched orders (in which buy and sell orders are made in rapid succession in order to give the impression of active trading), inducing trading by false statements, and the misuse of pro forma financial statements. In general, it discourages any fraudulent plot or scheme designed to manipulate the market for temporary advantage.[8]

To further protect the investor, any officer, director, or person who owns more than 10 percent of a registered company must file an initial report with the SEC as well as with the exchange where the relevant securities are traded, and the report must list any holdings of equity securities.[9] In addition, any person who acquires over 5 percent beneficial ownership[10] in stock that is registered under Section 12 of the 1934 Act also must provide selected information to the SEC within 10 days of the transaction or within 2 days if the percent beneficial ownership exceeds 10 percent.[11] Thereafter, reports must be filed on a timely basis whenever changes are made in the holdings of the officers, directors, or beneficial owners of the stock. Any gains on short-term transactions or on short sales may be recovered by the company or on its behalf by any of its security holders. This requirement discourages anyone from using confidential corporate (i.e., "inside") information for personal advantage in trading equity securities. A considerable amount of litigation has been enacted relating to trading on inside information, with the protection of the investor as a primary objective. Nevertheless, trading on inside information continues to be a problem in the regulation of the securities markets. For example, in June of 2003, securities fraud and related obstruction of justice charges were filed against one of America's domestic style icons, Martha Stewart, when she sold her holdings in ImClone Systems, Inc. stock after illegally receiving from a stockbroker inside information regarding stock sales by members of the company's management.[12]

Other Provisions. In regulating securities trading on the national exchanges, the 1934 Act has three other important provisions. The first is the authority to regulate proxy solicitation, for the election of directors or

---

8. United States, *Securities Exchange Act of 1934*, Sec. 10.
9. *Ibid.* Section 12(b)(1)(D).
10. Beneficial ownership is direct or indirect ownership and/or voting power.
11. *Ibid.* Section 13(d)(1).
12. United States, Securities and Exchange Commission, "SEC Charges Martha Stewart, Froker Peter Bacanovic with Illegal Insider Trading," Press Release 2003-69, 4 June 2003.

for approval of other corporate actions.[13] This provision is closely tied to the disclosure objective of the 1934 Act. Section 14(a) gives very broad power to the SEC by making it unlawful for anyone to solicit a proxy or consent except under the rules the SEC may establish for the protection of investors. The purpose of the proxy rule is to ensure that sufficient disclosures are made to permit an investor to use the right to vote intelligently. These proxy requirements are among the most effective disclosure rules in the area of securities laws.

In 1964 the SEC amended its proxy rules to require disclosure and reconciliation of any material differences in the application of accounting principles between reports filed with the SEC and reports provided the shareholders. This action was intended to discourage companies from telling the SEC one thing and the stockholders something different. The 1964 amendments proved to be very effective in reducing the discrepancies between the annual reports to shareholders and the reports submitted to the SEC.

A second provision calls for the disclosure of all pertinent information in tender offer solicitations. A tender offer solicitation is a bid in the form of a public invitation to shareholders to buy the stock they hold at a specified price. Before tender offers can be made, the prospective buyer must file with the SEC the following information: the principal business of the buyer, the source of funds to be used in the purchase, the purpose of the transaction, and the amount of equity securities to be purchased from shareholders. This regulation helps to prevent any surprise "take-over bids" and allows an issuer time to consider and respond to the tender offer.

A final provision of the 1934 Act authorizes the Board of Governors of the Federal Reserve System to control the use of margins in securities trading. Margin is the percentage of equity investment investors maintain in their brokerage account when purchasing securities with credit. Margin requirements can be raised or lowered, depending on whether the Federal Reserve desires to stimulate or to curtail investment. The SEC retains the responsibility of enforcing these margin restrictions in connection with its periodic review of the exchanges and brokers.

---

13. Proxy solicitation is the process by which investors or management can solicit shareholders for proxy voting rights at one or more shareholder meetings. Proxy solicitation is often used by management to garner support for measures, but it is also used by institutional investors to increase their voting power.

Enforcement Power.   The SEC is given broad enforcement powers under Section 12 of the 1934 Act. If the rules of operation for exchanges prove to be ineffectual in implementing the requirements of the SEC, the SEC can alter or supplement them. The SEC can suspend trading of a security for not more than 10 days (a series of orders has enabled the SEC to suspend trading for extended periods, however) and can suspend all trading on any exchange for up to 90 days. If hearings show that the issuer failed to comply with the requirements of the securities laws, the SEC can de-list any security. Brokers and dealers can be prevented, either temporarily or permanently, from working in the securities market. Investigations can be initiated if deemed necessary to determine violations of any of the Acts or rules administered by the SEC.

Effect of 1934 Act on Accountants.   Accountants can be censured and their work is subject to approval by the SEC. Accountants are involved in the preparation and review of a major portion of the reports and statements required by the 1934 Act. The financial statements in the annual report to stockholders and in the 10-K report must be audited by independent public accountants. In addition, accountants internal to the company consult and assist in the preparation of the quarterly 10-Q and other periodic reports, which are the result of many hours of work both by the accounting staff of the registrant and by its independent certifying auditors.

Since the SEC requires periodic reports from registered brokers and dealers, the books of these brokers and dealers must be thoroughly audited, and extensive financial reports must be prepared and certified by an independent public accountant. With the requirements of ASR No. 156 incorporated in current SEC requirements, accounting firms are also equipped to give expert assistance to brokers or dealers to ensure that they meet the strict record keeping and financial reporting requirements of the SEC.

In addition to the auditing of brokers' and dealers' books, another important area of concern for the accountant is proxy statements— documents sent to shareholders relaying information about issues on which investors are requested to vote. These statements generally must be accompanied and supported by certified financial statements. Again, accountants are expected to provide professional expertise in the proper preparation and documentation of these statements.

Finally, the Foreign Corrupt Practices Act of 1977, an amendment to the 1934 Act, further increased the responsibilities of accountants. The 1977 Act amended Section 13(b) of the 1934 Act to require those companies under SEC jurisdiction to maintain proper books, records, and accounts and a sufficient system of internal control. The Foreign Corrupt Practices Act of 1977 is discussed later in this chapter.

Sarbanes-Oxley Public Company Accounting Reform and
Investor Protection Act of 2002

In July of 2002, President George W. Bush signed into law the Sarbanes-Oxley Act of 2002 (the 2002 Act). As indicated in Chapter 1, the Sarbanes-Oxley Act was enacted in response to the scandals of 2001 and 2002, which cost American investors billions of dollars and severely shook investor confidence. The 2002 Act is considered the most sweeping securities law since the 1933 and 1934 Acts. Its main objectives are to restore investor confidence in the securities markets and to deter future corporate frauds from occurring.

Although Congress created and passed the 2002 Act, as is customary with similar legislation, Congress does not develop the specific detailed accounting and securities rules and regulations needed to execute the Act's provisions. Instead, the Act delegates substantial authority and responsibility to the SEC to create the rules and regulations necessary to implement the legislation. For example, Section 302 of the 2002 Act directed the SEC to create rules requiring CEO and CFO certification of periodic financial reports within 30 days of the legislation's signing. In August of 2002, the SEC implemented a final ruling based on this requirement.[14] This delegation of rule-making power by the Sarbanes-Oxley Act to the SEC occurs throughout the Act, as seen in Exhibit 3-1. This exhibit provides a section-by-section summary of the Act and outlines the actions taken by the SEC to execute the many different parts of the legislation. The table does not include all SEC rules and regulations related to the Act, since SEC rule making is concurrent with the writing of this book.

In some cases, the language of the 2002 Act is very general when directing the SEC to issue rules. In these situations, the SEC provides clarification and interpretation of the language of the Act. For example, Section 404 directs the SEC to issue rules requiring annual management

14. United States. Securities Exchange Commission, "Final Rule: Certification of Disclosure in Companies' Quarterly and Annual Reports," Release No. 33-8124, 29 Aug. 2002.

reports on the effectiveness of internal control over financial reporting. When final rules were issued by the SEC, it provided a lengthy definition of the term "internal control over financial reporting," recognizing the ambiguity of that particular phrase referred to in the Act.

Also, in some instances, the SEC's rules extend beyond what was required by the Act. For instance, Section 802 stipulates that audit firms must retain their audit work papers for a period of five years whereas the SEC ruling extends the period to seven years.

Creation of the Public Company Accounting Oversight Board. The Sarbanes-Oxley Act gives authority to the SEC to further delegate its regulatory powers. As illustrated in Exhibit 3-1, the very first section in the 2002 Act outlines the creation of the Public Company Accounting Oversight Board (PCAOB) to

> oversee the audit of public companies that are subject to the securities laws . . . in order to protect the interests of investors and further the public interest in the preparation of informative, accurate, and independent audit reports for companies the securities of which are sold to, and held by and for, public investors [Section 101(a)].

Congress believed that the AICPA's Auditing Standards Board, the previous auditing standards setter (for both private and public company audits), had not maintained autonomy or independence from the public-company auditors. Further, critics believed that the AICPA had become lax in its supervision and oversight of audit firms—partly because the AICPA is a private association sponsored by, and representing, the accounting profession and because the Auditing Standards Board included members who were concurrently serving in prominent positions with their audit firms.[15]

The PCAOB was established as a non-profit corporation designed to be independent from the accounting profession as a whole. The Board consists of five board members of which two, and only two, "shall be or have been certified public accountants." The SEC appoints the board's members and has direct oversight responsibilities over the PCAOB. The SEC declared the

---

15. David Katz, "Troubled Times at the AICPA." *CFO.com* 1 July 2003. Accessed 9 Sep. 2003 <http://www.cfo.com/Article?article=9882>.

Board fully organized and operational in April 2003. All public company auditors must now register with the PCAOB. The PCAOB has issued two standards by March 2004 with the most notable being its standard related to the audit of internal controls required by Sarbanes-Oxley Rule 404. In 2003 the PCAOB also began, on a test basis, examining the competency and sufficiency of public company audits.

Key duties of the PCAOB as set forth in Sections 101 through 106 of the Act include the following:

- Registering public accounting firms that prepare audit reports for publicly-traded companies,
- Establishing auditing, quality control, ethics, and independence standards for auditors,
- Conducting inspections of registered accounting firms,
- Conducting investigations and disciplinary proceedings of registered accounting firms, and
- Performing other duties necessary to promote high standards among registered accounting firms.

The 2002 Act gives the SEC substantial authority in both the formation of and ongoing operations of the Board. The SEC appoints Board members and designates terms of service [Section 101(e)]. The SEC also has authority to terminate a Board member.

Exhibit 3-1: Summary of Sarbanes-Oxley Act of 2002

Title I—Public Company Accounting Oversight Board		
Sec. **Title**	**SEC/Other Action**	**Action Date**
101 Establishment, administrative provisions	SEC declared PCAOB operational.	12/19/02
102 Registration with the board	PCAOB Release No. 2003-07: Registration System for Public Accounting Firms	5/6/03
103 Auditing, quality control, and independence standards and rules PCAOB actions regarding this responsibility will be ongoing.	PCAOB Release No. 2003-06: Establishment of Interim Professional Auditing Standards	4/18/03
104 Inspections of registered accounting firms	PCAOB Release No. 2003-019: Inspection of Registered Accounting Firms	10/7/03
105 Investigations and disciplinary proceedings	PCAOB Release No. 2003-015: Rules on Investigations and Adjudications	9/29/03
106 Foreign Public Accounting Firms	PCAOB Release No. 2003-024: Proposed Rule on Oversight of Non-US Firms	12/10/03
107 Commission Oversight of the Board The SEC approves all Board rules, reviews and can modify Board disciplinary actions, and has authority to censure or sanction the Board and censure and remove Board members, as necessary.	Ongoing oversight	
108 Accounting Standards SEC required to perform a study regarding the adoption of principles-based accounting standards	SEC Study Pursuant to Section 108(d) of the Sarbanes-Oxley Act of 2002	7/25/03
109 Funding	PCAOB Release No. 2003-003: Board Funding: Establishment of Accounting Support Fee	4/18/03

Title II—Auditor Independence			
Sec.	Title	SEC/Other Action	Action Date
201	Services Outside the Scope of Practice of Auditors	SEC Release No. 33-8183: Final Rule: Strengthening the Commission's Requirements Regarding Auditor Independence	1/28/03
202	Pre-approval Requirements	SEC Release No. 33-8183	1/28/03
203	Audit Partner Rotation	SEC Release No. 33-8183	1/28/03
204	Auditor Reports to Audit Committees	SEC Release No. 33-8183	1/28/03
205	Conforming Amendments	None necessary	N/A
206	Conflicts of Interest	SEC Release No. 33-8183	1/28/03
207	Study of Mandatory Rotation of Registered Public Accounting Firms	GAO Report 04-216: Public Accounting Firms: Required Study on the Potential Effects of Mandatory Audit Firm Rotation	11/21/03
208	Commission Authority Authorizes and requires SEC to issue regulations implementing auditor independence provisions of Title II	SEC Release No. 33-8183	1/28/03
209	Considerations by Appropriate State Regulatory Authorities	States are reconsidering their accounting and auditing related regulations.	N/A

Title III—Corporate Responsibility			
Sec.	**Title**	**SEC/Other Action**	**Action Date**
301	Public Company Audit Committees	SEC Release No. 33-8220: Standards Relating to Listed Company Audit Committees	4/9/03
302	Corporate Responsibility for Financial Reports Requires CEO/CFO certification of periodic reports filed with the SEC	SEC Release No. 33-8124: Certification of Disclosure in Companies' Quarterly and Annual Reports	8/29/02
303	Improper Influence on Conduct of Audits	SEC Release No. 34-47890: Improper Influence on Conduct of Audits	5/20/03
304	Forfeiture of Certain Bonuses and Profits	None necessary	N/A
305	Officer and Director Bars and Penalties	None necessary	N/A
306	Insider Trades During Pension Fund Blackout Periods	SEC Release No. 34-47225: Insider Trades During Pension Fund Blackout Periods	1/22/03
307	Rules of Professional Responsibility for Attorneys	SEC Release No. 33-8185: Implementation of Standards of Professional Conduct for Attorneys	1/29/03
308	Fair Funds for Investors	SEC Report: Report Pursuant to Section 308(c) of the Sarbanes-Oxley Act of 2002	1/24/03

Title IV—Enhanced Financial Disclosures

Sec.	Title	SEC/Other Action	Action Date
401	Disclosures in Periodic Reports (off-balance sheet section)	SEC Release No. 33-8182: Disclosure in Management's Discussion and Analysis about Off-Balance Sheet Arrangements and Aggregate Contractual Obligations SEC Release No. 33-8176: Conditions for Use of Non-GAAP Financial Measures	1/28/03; 1/22/03
402	Enhanced Conflict of Interest Provisions	None necessary	N/A
403	Disclosures of Transactions Involving Management and Principal Stockholders	SEC Release No. 34-46421: Ownership Reports and Trading by Officers, Directors and Principal Security Holders SEC Release No. 33-8230: Mandatory Electronic Filing and Web site Posting for Forms 3, 4 and 5	8/27/02 5/7/03
404	Management Assessment of Internal Controls Management is required to report on internal controls; auditor is required to issue attestation report on management's assertion.	SEC Release No. 33-8238: Management's Reports Over Internal Control Over Financial Reporting and Certification of Disclosure in Exchange Act Periodic Reports PCAOB Release 2003-017: Proposed Auditing Standard —An Audit of Internal Control Over Financial Reporting Performed in Conjunction with an Audit of Financial Statements	6/5/03 10/7/03

405	Exemption	None necessary	N/A
406	Code of Ethics for Senior Financial Officers	SEC Release No. 33-8177: Disclosure Required by Sections 406 and 407 of the Sarbanes-Oxley Act of 2002	1/23/03
407	Disclosure of Audit Committee Financial Expert	SEC Release No. 33-8177	1/23/03
408	Enhanced Review of Periodic Disclosures by Issuers	None necessary	N/A
409	Real Time Issuer Disclosures	SEC Release No. 33-8400: Additional Form 8-K Disclosure Requirements and Acceleration of Filing Date	03/16/04

Title V—Analyst Conflicts of Interest

Sec.	Title	SEC/Other Action	Action Date
501	Treatment of Securities Analysts by Registered Securities Associations and National Securities Exchanges	SEC Release No. 33-8193: Regulation Analyst Certification	2/20/03

Title VI—Commission Resources and Authority

Sec.	Title	SEC/Other Action	Action Date
601	Authorization by Appropriations	None necessary	N/A
602	Appearance and Practice Before the Commission	None necessary	N/A
603	Federal Court Authority to Impose Penny Stock Bars	SEC Proposed Rule 34-49037: Amendments to the Penny Stock Rules	1/8/04
604	Qualifications of Associated Persons of Brokers and Dealers	None necessary	N/A

Title VII—Studies and Reports

Sec.	Title	SEC/Other Action	Action Date
701	GAO Study and Report Regarding Consolidation of Public Accounting Firms	GAO Report 03-864: Public Accounting Firms: Mandated Study on Consolidation and Competition, GAO Report 03-1158: Accounting Firm Consolidation: Selected Large Public Company Views on Audit Fees, Quality, Independence, and Choice	7/30/03 9/30/03
702	Commission Study and Report Regarding Credit Rating Agencies	SEC Report: Report on the Role and Function of Credit Rating Agencies in the Operation of the Securities Markets	1/24/03
703	Study and Report on Violators and Violations	SEC Report: Study and Report on Violations by Securities Professionals	1/24/03
704	Study of Enforcement Actions	SEC Report: Report Pursuant to Section 704 of The Sarbanes-Oxley Act of 2002	1/24/03
705	Study of Investment Banks	GAO Report 03-511: Investment Banks: The Role of Firms and Their Analysts with Enron and Global Crossing	3/17/03

Title VIII—Corporate and Criminal Fraud Accountability			
Sec.	Title	SEC/Other Action	Action Date
801	Short Title	None necessary	N/A
802	Criminal Penalties for Altering Documents	SEC Release No. 33-8180: Retention of Records Relevant to Audits and Reviews	1/24/03
803	Debts Nondischargable if Incurred in Violation of Securities Fraud Laws	None necessary	N/A
804	Statute of Limitations for Securities Fraud	None necessary	N/A
805	Review of Federal Sentencing Guidelines for Obstruction of Justice and Extensive Criminal Fraud	2003 US Sentencing Commission Guidelines manual contains perm-anent increased penalties	11/1/03
806	Protection for Employees of Publicly Traded Companies who Provide Evidence of Fraud	None necessary	N/A
807	Criminal Penalties for Defrauding Shareholders of Publicly Traded Companies	None necessary	N/A

Title IX—White-collar Crime Penalty Enhancements			
Sec.	Title	SEC/Other Action	Action Date
901-6	White-Collar Crime Penalty Enhancements	US Sentencing Commission actions, as detailed above	1/25/03 11/1/03
1001	Corporate Tax Returns	None necessary	N/A
1101-7	Corporate Fraud Accountability	US Sentencing Commission actions, as detailed above	1/25/03 11/1/03

The 2002 Act allowed the PCAOB to decide whether it wanted to delegate audit standard-setting to the AICPA's Auditing Standards Board or to assume the standard-setting responsibility. In April of 2003, the PCAOB voted to adopt existing AICPA audit standards on an interim basis, but the board also decided that it would assume the standard-setting role for public-company audits. This decision represents a drastic change in the accounting profession because before April 2003, the auditing profession set auditing standards and was essentially "self-regulated." The PCAOB determined that the AICPA lacked the necessary independence and had proven ineffective at self-regulation; it will take years to determine if the PCAOB's standards help to restore public confidence and improve auditor performance.[16] Given the repeated history of prosperous economic times, excess and then abuse, corporate scandal, and reform, it seems more a question of "when" not "if" the next round of corporate scandals occur. When future audits fail to uncover massive fraud, the PCAOB and SEC will not be able to point to the AICPA or other professional association. Whether the next round of scandals results in a PCAOB replacement or a stronger, more far-reaching PCAOB remains to be seen.

Corporate Responsibility. Some of the most important provisions of the 2002 Act are aimed at increasing the responsibility of corporate officers and directors for the reliability of their companies' financial statements. The authors of the 2002 Act knew that the primary culprits in corporate fraud are dishonest officers and directors. Section 302 of the Act directs the SEC to adopt rules that require the chief executive and chief financial officers of each public company to personally certify in each annual or quarterly report filed with the SEC that:

- The signing officer has reviewed the report;
- Based on the officer's knowledge, the report does not contain any untrue statement of a material fact or omit to state a material fact necessary to make the statements not misleading;
- Based on the officer's knowledge, the financial statements and other information presented fairly present the financial conditions and operations of the issuer;

---

16. The AICPA also set accounting standards in the past, but a perceived lack of independence on the part of the AICPA led to the formation of the Financial Accounting Standards Board as the recognized standard setter in 1973.

- The signing officers:
  o Are responsible for establishing and maintaining internal controls,
  o Have designed the internal controls to ensure that material information relating to the issuer and its consolidated subsidiaries is made known to the officers by others within those entities,
  o Have evaluated the effectiveness of the issuer's internal controls within 90 days prior to the report, and
  o Have presented in the report their conclusions about the effectiveness of the internal controls based on their evaluation as of that date;
- The signing officers have disclosed to the issuer's auditors and audit committee:
  o All significant deficiencies in the design or operation in internal controls, and
  o Any fraud, material or immaterial, that involves management or other employees who have a significant role in the issuer's internal controls; and
- The signing officers have indicated in the report whether there were significant changes in internal controls or in other factors that could significantly affect internal controls.

Section 302 gave the SEC 30 days to adopt rules enforcing the section. On August 29, 2002, the SEC released the final ruling (No. 33-8124), "Certification of Disclosure in Companies' Quarterly and Annual Reports," which complies with Section 302. Section 302 is not the only section of the Act that requires a company's officers to make certifications. Section 404 of the 2002 Act requires certain additional management assertions regarding the effectiveness of internal controls, and Section 906 requires each periodic report containing financial statements filed with the SEC to contain certifications in addition to those required under Section 302. Section 906 requires CEOs and CFOs to certify that:

- The periodic report containing the financial statements fully complies with the requirements of Section 13(a) or 15(d) of the 1934 Act (see Chapter 4 for further information), and

- The information contained in the periodic report fairly presents, in all material respects, the financial condition and results of operations of the issuer.

Congress obviously intended to make it clear to corporate officers that the responsibility for fair presentation of their companies' financial statements rests squarely with them.

Section 303 of the Act requires the SEC to implement rules prohibiting "officers and directors of an issuer, and persons acting under the direction of an officer or director, from coercing, manipulating, misleading, or fraudulently influencing the auditor of the issuer's financial statements if that person knew or should have known that such action could render the financial statements materially misleading." In May of 2003, the SEC adopted rules to implement Section 303 (SEC Release No. 34-47890).

Section 402 also deals with corporate responsibility. This section prohibits public companies from extending personal loans to directors or officers except in a limited number of circumstances, such as home improvement and manufactured home loans, consumer credit, credit cards, and certain bank loans made in the ordinary course of the company's consumer credit business. Loans to officers, which were often later forgiven, was a common abuse in the scandals of 2000–2002. Perhaps the most notorious "loan" program was at Tyco International, where executives, including CEO Dennis Kozlowski, CFO Mark Swartz, and Tyco general counsel Mark Belnick, were given loans totaling tens of millions of dollars.

Enhanced Disclosure Requirements. In an effort to increase the transparency of financial statements, the 2002 Act includes several provisions expanding and enhancing financial statement disclosures. Section 401 states,

> each financial report filed with the SEC containing financial information prepared in accordance with (or reconciled to) generally accepted accounting principles . . . must reflect all material correcting adjustments that have been identified by a registered public accounting firm . . . .

Section 401 also directs the SEC to issue, within 180 days of the Act's signing, rules requiring that each annual and quarterly financial report must disclose all material off-balance sheet transactions, arrangements, contingent obligations, and other relationships with unconsolidated entities that may have a material effect on the company. This provision was undoubtedly in response to Enron's infamous abuses of off-balance sheet techniques. However, the SEC rule implementing this section (SEC Release No. 33-8182) contains a subtle difference in wording. The SEC requires companies to disclose off-balance sheet transactions that would be "reasonably likely" to have a material effect on the company, instead of transactions that "may have" a material effect. The SEC's less stringent wording eases the time and cost burden of compliance for companies with multiple, small legitimate off-balance sheet items (particularly financial institutions).

Section 401 of the 2002 Act also directs the SEC to issue rules concerning pro forma reports. Pro forma reports predict future financial performance based on certain specified expectations and assumptions (e.g., "if a new product performs as expected"). The SEC issued final rulings in January 2003 (SEC Release No. 33-8176), "providing that pro forma financial information included in any periodic or other report filed with the SEC pursuant to the securities laws . . . shall be presented in a manner that—

- Does not contain an untrue statement of a material fact or omit to state a material fact necessary in order to make the pro forma financial information . . . not misleading, and
- Reconciles it with the financial condition and results of operations of the issuer under generally accepted accounting principles" [Section 401(b)].

Under direction of the Act, the SEC modified earlier rules relating to insiders—directors, executive officers, and stockholders owning 10 percent or more of a class of securities. In the past, insiders had to file Form 4 within the first 10 days of the calendar month following a reportable transaction. The SEC's rule implementing Section 403 now requires insiders to file Form 4 within two business days following a reportable transaction. This rule took effect in August of 2002.

Perhaps the most ambitious set of disclosure enhancements of the 2002 Act relates to internal controls. As noted above, corporate executives are required to establish, maintain, and certify that their company's controls are effective for reporting on internal control. Section 404(b) of the Act also requires the public accounting firm preparing the audit report for a given company's 10-K to attest to and report on the internal control report prepared by management. The SEC issued final rules regarding Section 404 in June of 2003 (SEC Release No. 33-8238), which require additional disclosures to those mentioned in Section 404 of the Act. In addition to disclosing management's responsibility for internal control and management's assessment of that internal control, companies will have to disclose the following:

- A statement identifying the framework used by management to evaluate the effectiveness of this internal control; and
- A statement that the company's auditor has issued an attestation report on management's assessment.

Under the SEC's final ruling, management must disclose any "material weakness(es)" in internal controls. The existence of any material weaknesses means that there is no basis for concluding that the company's system of internal control over financial reporting is effective. The framework management uses to establish and evaluate its internal controls must be a recognized control framework established by a body or group that has followed due-process procedures, including open deliberations and public comment.[17] The SEC's ruling also requires companies to perform quarterly evaluations of changes that materially affect the company's internal control. Recognizing the amount of time required for companies to comply with the requirements implementing Section 404, the SEC final ruling delayed the date to June 2004 for company compliance. However, in February 2004, the deadline for compliance was further delayed. The deadline for complying varies depending on fiscal year and filing status but it begins as early as November 15, 2004, and by July 15, 2005, all companies must comply.[18] Estimates of the cost to U.S. public companies to implement, validate, and certify internal controls as required by Section 404 range from $50,000 to $10 million, according to a "GAIN Flash Survey" conducted by the Institute of Internal Auditors in October, 2003. Section 404 also dramatically increases the time and effort required by public accounting firms, which

---

17. United States, Securities and Exchange Commission, "SEC Implements Internal Control Provisions of Sarbanes-Oxley Act," Press Release 2003-66, 27 May 2003.
18. For deadline details, see SEC Release No. 33-8392, "Management's Report on Internal Control over Financial Reporting and Certification of Disclosure in Exchange Act Periodic Reports," 24 Feb. 2004.

obviously translates to higher fees. While improved internal controls will certainly provide benefits, it remains to be seen if the benefits of internal control certification and attestation exceed the costs.

The SEC implemented section 409 of the Sarbanes-Oxley Act through its Final Ruling 33-8400 (March 16, 2004). This ruling expands the listing of events that trigger the need for a Form 8-K filing and speeds up the 8-K filing deadline. The 8-K filing changes are discussed in greater detail in Chapter 5.

Other disclosures required by the 2002 Act relate to codes of ethics and audit committees. Section 406 of the Act directs the SEC to issue rules requiring public companies to disclose in periodic reports whether they have adopted a code of ethics for senior financial officers and, if not, why not. The Act stipulates that codes of ethics should relate to such things as conflicts of interest, accurate and understandable disclosures in periodic reports, and compliance with governmental rules and regulations. In January of 2003, the SEC adopted rules requiring companies to disclose code of ethics information in their periodic reports (*SEC Release No. 33-8177*). The SEC final ruling expands the provision in Section 406 by requiring disclosure about codes of ethics for its "principal executive" and not just senior financial officers.[19]

Section 407 directs the SEC to issue rules requiring disclosures about audit committees. Specifically, companies are to disclose "whether or not, and if not, the reasons therefore, the audit committee . . . is comprised of at least one member who is a financial expert, as such term is defined by the Commission" [Section 407(a)]. The SEC defined the term "financial expert" to mean,

> a person who has, through education and experience as a public accountant, auditor, principal financial officer, controller or principal accounting officer, of a company that, at the time the person held such position, was required to file reports pursuant to Section 13(a) or 15(d) of the Exchange Act, or experience in one or more positions that involve the performance of similar functions (or that results, in the judgment of the company's board of directors, in the person's having similar expertise and experience), the following attributes:

---

19. United States, Securities and Exchange Commission, "Final Rule: Disclosure Required by Sections 406 and 407 of the Sarbanes-Oxley Act of 2002," Release No. 33-8177, 23 Jan. 2003.

- An understanding of generally accepted accounting principles and financial statements;
- Experience applying such generally accepted accounting principles in connection with the accounting for estimates, accruals, and reserves that are generally comparable to the estimates, accruals and reserves, if any, used in the registrant's financial statements;
- Experience preparing or auditing financial statements that present accounting issues that are generally comparable to those raised by the registrant's financial statements;
- Experience with internal controls and procedures for financial reporting; and
- An understanding of audit committee functions.[20]

The SEC ruling on Section 407 also requires companies to disclose whether the financial expert is independent of management.

After the SEC enacted regulations putting Sections 406 and 407 in place, the business community expressed confusion over whether the SEC required these new disclosures in registration statements under both the 1933 and 1934 Acts. The SEC clarified companies needed to provide information regarding their financial experts only in the annual report, regulated by the 1934 Act.[21]

Effects of Sarbanes-Oxley Act on Public Accountants. The 2002 Act imposes far-reaching restrictions and regulations on public company auditors. The three largest effects are (1) the creation of the Public Company Accounting Oversight Board to oversee audits of public companies, (2) the internal control attestation required by Section 404, and (3) restrictions on consulting and non-audit services. We have already discussed (1) and (2); in this section we focus on restrictions to non-audit services as well as other aspects of the 2002 Act that directly effect public accountants.

Section 201 deals with non-audit services. For decades a debate has raged over whether the provision of consulting services for audit clients by

---

20. Ibid.
21. United States, Securities and Exchange Commission, "Correction to Final Rule: Disclosure Required by Sections 406 and 407 of the Sarbanes-Oxley Act of 2002," Release No. 33-8177A, 26 Mar. 2003.

public accounting firms compromised auditor objectivity and independence. In the wake of the scandals of 2000–2002, this debate came to a culmination in the Sarbanes-Oxley Act as witnesses declared in congressional hearings that public-company auditors were soft on clients that also engaged the firm to provide lucrative consulting services. It had become common for consulting fees paid to the public accounting firm to be greater than the audit fee itself (as was the case with Andersen's fees from Enron, for example). Performing non-audit services was alleged to have impaired the auditors' objectivity and ability to take tough stands against aggressive clients, for fear of losing the consulting fees. Whatever the reasons, what is clear is that auditors issued clean audit opinions on materially misstated financial statements, and when the truth was revealed, investors lost billions. Congress, in an attempt to increase auditors' objectivity and willingness to confront aggressive clients, wrote Section 201 prohibiting public-company auditor firms from providing the following services for audit clients:

- Bookkeeping and related services
- Financial information systems design and implementation
- Appraisal or valuation services, fairness opinions
- Actuarial services
- Internal audit outsourcing services
- Management functions or human resources
- Broker or dealer, investment adviser, or investment banking services
- Legal services and expert services unrelated to the audit

All other non-audit services, including tax services, are permissible only if the client's audit committee pre-approves the service.

Section 203 of the Act requires audit partner (although not audit firm) rotation. The lead audit partner and/or the concurring review partner must rotate off the engagement if he or she has performed audit services for the issuer in each of the five previous fiscal years. The SEC final ruling on this section added the requirement that once partners rotate off a client engagement, they have a five-year "time-out" period before they can work on the engagement again.[22] This part of the Act will cause significant

---

22. United States, Securities and Exchange Commission, "Final Rule: Strengthening the Commission's Requirements Regarding Auditor Independence," Release No. 33-8183, 28 Jan. 2003.

scheduling difficulties as the domino effect of rotating partners impacts client and office partner assignments—particularly for smaller offices. Recognizing the burden partner rotation would place on small audit firms, the SEC exempts firms with less than ten partners and less than five public company audit clients from the requirement, provided they undergo reviews by the PCAOB every three years.

Section 206 of the Act requires significant improvement in the communication between auditors and audit committees. The Act requires auditors to provide audit committees with the following information:

- Reports regarding critical accounting policies,
- Alternative GAAP treatments discussed with management and the implications of those treatments—including the treatment preferred by the accounting firm, and
- Other material written communications, such as management letters and schedules of unadjusted differences (i.e., listings of errors found by auditors and left uncorrected by management).

Section 206 provides rules relating to conflicts of interest between audit firms and their clients. This section prohibits registered accounting firms from performing an audit if the CEO, CFO, chief accounting officer, or controller of the issuer was employed by the accounting firm and participated in the audit of that issuer during the one-year period preceding initiation of the audit. This section, similar to sections 201 and 203 of the Act, seeks to keep auditors as objective and independent as possible.

Although the Sarbanes-Oxley Act affects accountants and auditors in many ways, accountants should anticipate future rules that will further regulate the profession. The Act calls for several studies to be conducted, some of which may directly affect the accounting profession in the future. One such study will explore the feasibility of changing to a system of "principles-based" accounting standards (as opposed to the current approach based on detailed rules) and another will examine the potential effects of mandatory audit firm rotation. The accounting profession has already gone through a whirlwind of change since 2002, and this trend will likely continue for some time to come.

OTHER IMPORTANT ACTS

In addition to the principal Acts—the Securities Act of 1933, the Securities Exchange Act of 1934, and the Sarbanes-Oxley Act of 2002—there are other important Acts that relate to the SEC and are important to businesses and to the public in general. These other Acts include: the Public Utility Holding Company Act of 1935; the Trust Indenture Act of 1939; the Investment Company Act of 1940; the Investment Advisers Act of 1940; the Securities Investor Protection Act of 1970; the Foreign Corrupt Practices Act of 1977; the Insider Trading Sanctions Act of 1984; the Private Securities Litigation Reform Act of 1995; and the Fair Disclosure Act of 2000.

Public Utility Holding Company Act of 1935[23]

In 1928, the Federal Trade Commission (FTC) began a thorough review of the practices and organizational structure of the utilities industry. The FTC uncovered a system of huge utility empires controlling widely scattered subsidiaries that had little or no economical or functional relationship to each other. Such companies were pyramided together, layer upon layer, and possessed very complex capital structures developed to utilize financial leverage and to reduce equity investment. This investigation led to passage of the Public Utility Holding Company Act of 1935, which established requirements for physical integration and corporate simplification of holding company systems.

Section 11(a) of the 1935 Act assigns responsibilities to the SEC

> to determine the extent to which the corporate structure . . . may be simplified, unnecessary complexities therein eliminated, voting power fairly and equitably distributed . . . and the properties and business thereof confined to those necessary or appropriate to the operations of an integrated public utility system.

The result has been a geographic integration, by which the SEC subdivided nearly all the utility empires, and a simplification of the capital structure of virtually all utility companies. The goal of the SEC was to create simple, coordinated systems confined to a single area or region and limited in such a way as not to impair the advantages of localized management, efficient operation, and effective regulation.

---

23. *The Work of the SEC, op. cit.,* 16-18.

The 1935 Act also empowers the SEC to regulate the terms and form of securities issued by utility companies. A reasonable capital structure is thereby maintained and competition is ensured among investment banks for underwriting and other services rendered to utility companies. Annual reports are submitted to keep the SEC current on the activities of registered companies. The 1935 Act also gives the SEC power to regulate the accounting systems of registered companies, to approve any acquisition or disposition of securities and assets, and to regulate intercompany transactions, such as loans and dividend payments.

Trust Indenture Act of 1939[24]

The Trust Indenture Act of 1939 stipulates that bonds, debentures, notes, and other debt securities offered for public sale can be issued only under a trust indenture approved by the SEC with a trustee appointed to protect the interests of investors in these securities. The Act generally applies to debt securities that are issued pursuant to trust indentures under which more than $7.5 million of securities are outstanding at any one time. There are provisions, however, that partially or totally exempt debt securities if they fall under established ceiling limitations. Because some issuers had failed to provide trustees who were capable of performing adequately on purchasers' behalf, the law was passed to protect these investors. The Act requires a trustee to be an independent corporation (free of conflicting interest) with minimum capitalization requirements. The registration form used under the 1939 Act requires disclosure of the indenture provisions and other information, allowing the SEC to rule on the capability of the trustee to serve successfully.

There are no requirements for certification of financial data contained in annual reports under this Act, but it is desirable to have an accountant review the indenture before it becomes final, since it could contain restrictions that the accountant needs to understand in order to serve a company adequately.

Investment Company Act of 1940[25]

The Investment Company Act of 1940 resulted from a comprehensive, four-year investigation of investment companies and investment advisors. The

---

24. Ibid., 19-20.
25. Ibid., 21-22.

investigation was made by the SEC pursuant to the direction of Congress. The Act, supported by the SEC and the industry, may be the most complex statute administered by the SEC. It regulates the activities of companies engaged primarily in investing, reinvesting, and trading in securities as well as those companies whose own securities are offered to the investing public. Registration under the 1940 Act is very similar to that under the 1933 and 1934 Acts, although registration under the 1940 Act does not eliminate the requirement for registration under the other Acts. Additionally, disclosure of the financial condition and investment policies of the company is required; this gives investors access to complete information concerning the activities of investment companies. All the disclosures must be updated periodically with reports sent to the SEC.

Other provisions prohibit: (1) investment companies from substantially changing the nature of their business or policies without stockholder approval; (2) persons guilty of securities fraud from serving as officers and directors; (3) underwriters, investment bankers, or brokers from constituting more than a minority of the board of directors; (4) transactions between the companies and their directors, officers, or affiliated companies or persons without prior SEC approval; (5) the issuance of securities senior to existing securities except under certain circumstances; and (6) pyramids of such companies and cross-ownership of their securities.

The registration statements and reports of regulated investment companies contain detailed financial statements and schedules—which must be certified by independent public accountants who must be elected by stockholders or appointed by directors and ratified by stockholders. The accountant also must conduct periodic, unannounced examinations of the securities held by investment companies and report the results to the SEC.

Investment Advisers Act of 1940[26]

The Investment Advisors Act of 1940 establishes a pattern of regulation for investment advisers that is similar to the conduct required of brokers and dealers under the 1934 Securities Exchange Act. With certain exceptions, the Investment Advisors Act requires persons or firms engaging in the business of advising others concerning their securities transactions to register with the SEC and to conform their activities to statutory standards designed to protect investors.

---

26. Ibid., 23.

This law requires proper and complete disclosure of information about investment advisers, their backgrounds, business affiliation, and bases for compensation. If the proper disclosure is not made by investment advisers, the SEC has the power either to deny registration or to suspend or revoke existing registration. The SEC may initiate injunctions or recommend prosecution of advisers for willful violations of securities laws. The SEC is also empowered to issue rules defining fraudulent practices that will not be tolerated.

A balance sheet, certified by an independent accountant, as well as other financial statements specified by the SEC must accompany the registration of investment advisors. In addition, accountants likely will be involved in preparing and maintaining the extensive records and accounts required by this Act, and in examining the securities held by investment advisers on behalf of their clients. Such an examination must be conducted annually and must be done without prior notice to the investment advisor. The results of the examination are to be reported to the SEC.

Securities Investor Protection Act of 1970

When the SEC learned that investors had suffered sizable losses in securities markets because of the financial difficulties of brokers and dealers, Congress enacted the Securities Investor Protection Act of 1970 as an amendment to the Securities Exchange Act of 1934. The 1970 Act created the Securities Investor Protection Corporation (SIPC), a non-profit organization whose membership comprises the brokers and dealers registered under Section 15(b) of the 1934 Act and members of the national securities exchanges. Five of the seven-member board of directors are appointed by the president of the United States, one by the Secretary of the Treasury, and one by the Federal Reserve Board. Two of the seven members may not be associated with the securities industry.

The SIPC creates a fund by collecting fees from the membership. These funds are used for the protection of investors who have investments with brokerage firms that close due to bankruptcy or financial distress. When a brokerage firm shuts down, the SIPC handles the distribution of securities to account holders, and reimburses investors for any other outstanding claims to a limit of $500,000 for each account and a maximum of $100,000 in cash claims for each account. The SIPC is required to file annual reports and financial statements with the SEC, and the SEC can make inspections of all SIPC activities.[27]

Foreign Corrupt Practices Act of 1977

Effective December 19, 1977, the Foreign Corrupt Practices Act (FCPA) was passed by Congress to control questionable or illegal foreign payments by U.S. companies. Under provisions of the Act, all companies in the United States and their officers, directors, employees, agents, or stockholders are prohibited from bribing foreign governmental or political officials. Foreign bribery is defined as "payments, or the offering of anything of value," to foreign officials as a means of promoting business interests. "Facilitating" or "grease" payments to relatively low-level government officials are not considered corrupt practices. An example of an acceptable practice is a payment to expedite shipments through customs or to secure required permits or licenses. Such payments are not viewed as impacting the higher-level decisions to secure a contract or otherwise increase business, but to facilitate transactions not involving discretionary action. For such payments to be allowed, and not considered illegal, the foreign officials' functions must be "essentially ministerial or clerical."

A second important element of the FCPA is the requirement that all public companies must: (1) keep reasonably detailed records that "accurately and fairly" reflect company financial activities, and (2) devise and maintain a system of internal accounting controls sufficient, among other things, to provide reasonable assurance that transactions are properly authorized, recorded, and accounted for. These two provisions are amendments to Section 13(b) of the Securities Exchange Act of 1934. Therefore, these provisions are applicable to all publicly held companies, not just those companies with foreign operations. All companies with securities registered under Section 12 of the 1934 Act and companies required to file periodic reports pursuant to Section 15(d) of the 1934 Act come under the legal requirements of the FCPA.

Although the record keeping and internal control provisions were intended to strengthen the anti-bribery provisions of the FCPA, the law does not limit the application of the provisions to detection or prevention of foreign bribery. Companies found guilty of making bribes, or which are otherwise not in compliance with the FCPA, may be subject to fines of up to

27. Louis Rappaport, *SEC Accounting Practice and Procedure*. 3rd ed. (New York: Ronald Press, 1972), 1.8–1.9.

$2 million; officers, directors, or employees may be fined up to $100,000 or imprisoned up to five years, or both.

The responsibility of accountants employed within companies to establish good accounting records and systems of internal control was not new; neither was the responsibility of independent accountants to assist in those functions and to review the internal control system as an essential part of conducting an audit. However, the FCPA, through the amendment to the 1934 Securities Act, subjects companies (including accountants) to civil liability and criminal prosecution under federal securities laws. The external auditor should be aware of the FCPA's provisions and should communicate to management and the audit committee any FCPA violations discovered during the audit work. This significant Act increases the responsibility of both internal and external accountants.

Insider Trading Sanctions Act of 1984 and Insider Trading and Securities Fraud Enforcement Act of 1988

On August 10, 1984, the Insider Trading Sanctions Act became law. Subsequently, on November 19, 1988, the Insider Trading and Securities Fraud Enforcement Act of 1988 was passed by Congress. These Acts substantially increase the penalties against persons who profit from illegal use of insider information. Formerly, the SEC could seek to recover only such gains. Now the SEC can seek fines of up to the greater of $1 million or three times the profits gained or losses avoided by those insiders who inappropriately use material, nonpublic information. The Acts also increase the criminal penalties associated with market manipulation, securities fraud, and other violations. Individuals now can be fined up to $1 million and receive jail sentences of up to 10 years. The laws do not define explicitly "material insider information," nor do they limit prohibitions to corporate insiders. Rather, anyone who aids another person in violating the insider trading rules may be held liable.

Private Securities Litigation Reform Act of 1995 and the Securities Litigation Uniform Standards Act of 1998

On December 22, 1995, Congress overrode a presidential veto and enacted the Private Securities Litigation Reform Act of 1995. This act made significant changes to securities fraud litigation, introduced proportionate liability, and created new responsibilities for auditors to detect and report illegal activities. Before Congress passed this act, auditors sued in federal courts (usually for allegedly failing to meet their responsibilities under the 1933 or 1934 Acts) were held to the legal doctrine of "joint and several liability," which holds each defendant liable for the full amount of the damages—even if the court deems them to be in reality only partially responsible for the plaintiff's losses. Plaintiffs, recognizing accounting and securities firms to have "deep pockets" had an incentive to create frivolous lawsuits against the firms, hoping to get large settlements. Oftentimes, following a sudden drop in a company's stock price, plaintiffs claimed the issuer and its auditors were at fault. The defendants would often settle to avoid going to court, paying hundreds of thousands of dollars in legal costs, and facing the risk of paying even more if a jury found them even partially responsible. The Reform Act introduced "proportionate liability," where each defendant was liable only for the share of the damages for which it was deemed responsible. However, "joint and several liability" still applies when it can be proven that a defendant knowingly violated the securities laws. The Act also required plaintiffs to present stronger reasons for their lawsuits prior to court proceedings than they had to in the past.

The Litigation Reform Act of 1995 only addressed liability in suits filed under federal law. The result was that plaintiffs' attorneys began to sue under various state laws, because some states still follow the joint and several liability standards. However, Congress addressed these attempts to circumvent the 1995 law in the 1998 Securities Litigation Uniform Standards Act. The 1998 Act provides that class action lawsuits alleging fraud regarding publicly traded securities (which are almost always traded across state lines) cannot be based on state law. The Act also provides that class action lawsuits filed in state courts regarding these "covered securities" can be dismissed or removed to a federal district court under certain circumstances.

Regulation FD

In 2000, the SEC adopted Regulation FD (for "fair disclosure"), which was intended to level the playing field in securities markets. The regulation applies to virtually all public companies, and it states that when issuers disclose material non-public information to groups such as securities analysts and institutional investors, the issuer needs to make simultaneous public disclosure of that information. The SEC believes that the "selective disclosure" that occurs when analysts and large investors get access to information before the general public closely resembles insider trading. In its release on Regulation FD, the SEC stated that selective disclosure also creates conflicts of interest for securities analysts who have an incentive to avoid making negative statements about a company out of fear of losing access to selectively disclosed information.

The timing of the public disclosure depends on whether the disclosure was intentional or unintentional. If the disclosure was intentional, the issuer needs to make public disclosure simultaneously. However, if the disclosure was unintentional, the issuer needs to disclosure the information within 24 hours after the company learns of the disclosure or before the start of the next trading day.

Prior to adoption of the Fair Disclosure rule, the SEC received more than 6,000 comment letters, mostly from individual investors. Not surprisingly, individual investors and the media generally favored the proposed regulation, believing that it would level the playing field for the retail investor. Large brokerage firms, on the other hand, generally opposed the rule, predicting that it would lead to a chilling of the information flow from issuers to the marketplace.[28] To date, most of the emerging academic research suggests that there has not been a chilling effect.[29] The number of advance statements of advance announcement of earnings, information often previously leaked only to analysts, has more than doubled since the adoption of Regulation FD, an indication of increased public information-sharing.[30] However, company policies as a result of this regulation vary from having a communications review procedure that is followed before making any outside communication, to announcing all data publicly through simulcasts or press releases.[31] Regulation FD applies only to disclosures by a company's senior management, its investor relations personnel, and others who routinely communicate with market professionals. The regulation does not apply to communications to the media or to securities rating agencies and it does not apply to routine business communications with customers and suppliers.

---

28. Laura Unger, "Special Study: Regulation Fair Disclosure Revisited," Securities and Exchange Commission, Dec. 2001.

29. For example, see F. Heflin, K. R. Subramanyam, and Yuan Zang, "Regulation FD and the Financial Information Environment: Early Evidence." *The Accounting Review* 78 (1) (2003): 1–37; V. Straser, "Regulation Fair Disclosure and Information Assymetry," University of Notre Dame, working paper (2002); A. Gintschel, and S. Markov, "The Effectiveness of Regulation FD," Deutsche Bank AG and Emory University, working paper (2003).

30. Ed. McCarthy, "Regulation FD: Coping in the Trenches," *Journal of Accountancy*, June 2003, p. 2.

31. Ibid. 4–6.

Regulation NMS (National Market System)

The Commission released proposed rule 34-49325 "Regulation NMS" in February 2004, and a final rule based on public comment and the proposed standard is likely to follow. Regulation NMS is a proposed "modernization" of portions of the Securities Exchange Act of 1934 that relate to the national market system (NMS). The proposed rule states, "We recognize that, if ultimately adopted, the rule proposals would effect fundamental innovations in the nation's equity markets. Today's action is intended to advance the dialogue on these vitally important market structure issues."

The key changes being proposed in Regulation NMS are,

1. the implementation of a uniform "trade-through" rule for national market centers that would ensure price priority (i.e., prevent securities being sold for less than the highest price posted at any national exchange),

2. a modernization of market access rules which should provide low-cost access to the best prices displayed in the NMS market centers,

3. a prohibition against using prices in the NMS in increments finer than a penny, except for stocks with a dollar value of less than $1.00, and

4. modification of rules for dissemination of NMS market center information to the public that changes the way fee revenue is shared to reward markets who contribute best to public price discovery.

SUMMARY

The reader who has carefully reviewed this survey of the legal framework of the SEC will be impressed by the broad powers delegated to the SEC to control the activities and to monitor the reports of the majority of business enterprises in the United States. Despite periodic criticisms, the SEC has been applauded as one of the most effective government agencies for its ability to improve the extent and accuracy of financial statement and other marketplace disclosures and for its ability to monitor and regulate the securities markets in the best interest of the investing public. The wide range of the SEC's activities and powers makes it an influential member of the business community. The SEC's influence continues to expand because of the need to monitor an increasing number of publicly traded companies and to protect a growing body of investors

DISCUSSION QUESTIONS

1. Name the primary Acts governed by the SEC.

2. What are the basic objectives of the Securities Act of 1933? How are these objectives being met?

3. List the major exemptions from registration under the 1933 Act, and list the categories in which they fall.

4. What is a comfort letter? Why is one issued in connection with a registration statement?

5. What did Congress attempt to do by passing the Securities Exchange Act of 1934? What agency was established by this Act?

6. Among the measures provided to protect the outside investor are certain restrictions on insiders. What are these restrictions?

7. Explain what a proxy is. What are the proxy solicitation requirements?

8. What new regulatory organization was created with the passage of the Sarbanes-Oxley Act of 2002? Describe the makeup of this organization. Name three key duties of this organization.

9. What aspects of the Sarbanes-OxleyAct most influence public-company executives? What aspects most influence public-company auditors?

10. With the passage of the Sarbanes-Oxley Act, what types of services are accounting firms prohibited from providing? Why?

11. What requirements are imposed by the Sarbanes-Oxley Act to increase the responsibility of corporate officers and directors?

12. What are the major purposes of the Investment Company Act of 1940 and the Investment Advisers Act of 1940?

13. Why is the word "foreign" in the title "Foreign Corrupt Practices Act of 1977" somewhat misleading?

4

SEC Registration and Reporting

In the previous chapter, each of the Acts endowing the SEC with its authority was explained. The purpose of this chapter is to examine the process of SEC registration, including some of the reporting requirements involved, and to describe the SEC's integrated disclosure system and filing system.

The rapid growth in business activity over the past 50 years, both within the United States and on a global scale, has brought a concurrent increase in the need for companies to seek capital to finance expansion. Much of this capital is obtained from public investment. The table in Exhibit 4-1 shows that the SEC's work is still considerable even though the total number of issuer reviews performed by the SEC has declined somewhat between 1998 and 2002.

Exhibit 4-1: Filings Reviewed by the SEC (1998-2002)

The following table summarizes the principal filings reviewed during the last five years.

Full Disclosure Reviews					
	1998	1999	2000	2001	2002
Major Filing Reviews					
Securities Act filings					
Initial Public Offerings	1,320	1,010	1,350	745	610
Repeat Issuers	720	510	270	620	715
P/E Amdts.[a]	28	10	10	25	15
Regulation A	81	65	70	50	30
Exchange Act					
Initial Registrations	338	680	1015	400	310
Annual Report Reviews					
Full[b]	1,527	1,375	595	880	1,220
Full Financial	997	960	550	1,400	1,440
Tender Offers (14D-1)	259	355	300	225	210
Going Private Schedules	115	180	115	145	90
Contested Proxy					
Solicitations	59	70	90	58	66
Proxy Statements					
Merger/Going Private	219	195	75	65	45
Others w/Financials	257	190	150	90	125
Reporting Issuer Reviews[c]	2,828	2,550	1,535	2,400	2,570
New Issuer Reviews[d]	1,739	1,755	2,435	1,195	950
Total Issuer Reviews	4,567	4,305	3,970	3,595	3,520

a. Post-effective amendments with new financial statements.
b. Includes annual reports reviewed in connection with the review of other filings that incorporated financial statements by reference.
c. Includes companies subject to Exchange Act reporting whose financial statements were reviewed during the year.
d. Includes reviews of Securities Act of 1933 registration statements and Exchange Act registrations by non-Exchange Act reporting companies. Includes reviews of Regulation A filings.

Source: <http://www.sec.gov/pdf/annrep02/ar02full.pdf>

Each SEC filing is accompanied by a myriad of documents and schedules, and each filing proceeds through the very detailed registration and review process explained in this chapter. As this process is explained, the reader should gain a new appreciation for the task of registrants in filing and the SEC in reviewing several thousand registrations each year.

THE REGISTRATION PROCESS: AN OVERVIEW

In reviewing the registration process and the SEC reporting requirements, one must keep in mind that the SEC's intent is not to judge the merits of securities offered for sale. A security may be a poor investment, but so long as information is presented fairly, the SEC will not prevent the sale of the security. Furthermore, the SEC's review process does not guarantee completeness or accuracy in the reports filed with the SEC. The securities laws provide for the disclosure of material financial and other information. They also impose severe penalties for presenting false and misleading information and for committing other fraudulent acts. The SEC's role is to determine if the evidence presented in the filed reports indicates satisfactory compliance with the applicable statutes and regulations, but the Commission's reviews are far from fail-safe. The system of financial reporting depends heavily on personal responsibility and accountability, effective corporate governance practices, and thorough financial statement audits by independent accountants. Any deficiencies are the responsibility of the company and the individuals involved (management, underwriters, attorneys, accountants, etc.). The final judgment on the investment opportunity presented by the offering rests with the potential investor.

A second important point is that SEC registration involves a significant amount of effort and expense.[1] Registration is a detailed, often lengthy process. With adequate disclosure being the main objective, registration requires simultaneous attention in several areas. Like a juggler attempting to keep several objects flying in the air at once, the registration process requires a company's management to coordinate several tasks simultaneously. Some companies are adept and successful at making registration a smooth process, while others fumble with one or two items, thus causing registration to become a series of starts and stops.

---

1. Wayne Kolins, *Guide to Going Public* (New York: Seidman & Seidman/BDO, 1987).

Not only is the initial registration process a complicated and time-consuming task, but the continuous reporting requirements and related costs of being a "public company" may be substantial. Extra accounting and legal work, at increased rates, are generally required for submitting the periodic SEC reports (e.g., Forms 8-K, 10-K, and 10-Q). It is quite common for public companies to maintain personnel who specialize in fulfilling SEC reporting requirements. Also, the SEC now requires electronic submission of essentially all reports and related materials, and there are intrinsic costs related to learning and adhering to these submission requirements.[2] The SEC's integrated disclosure system, explained in the next section of this chapter, is designed to streamline the reporting process and thereby reduce these reporting costs. Even with this integration, however, the increased responsibilities and costs of becoming and remaining a public company are significant.

Registration requirements are a major part of the specific Acts administered by the SEC. With some variations due to the differing purposes of the Acts, the registration processes required under the various Acts are still quite similar in terms of disclosure requirements and procedures. In review, the following list includes various Acts with general registration requirements:

- Securities Act of 1933: Registration of new securities offered for public sale.
- Securities Exchange Act of 1934: Registration of many market players (including exchanges, brokerage firms, clearing agencies, and self-regulatory organizations, such as the National Association of Securities Dealers,). Also, regular periodic reporting by publicly owned companies.
- Public Utility Holding Company Act of 1935: Registration of interstate holding companies covered by this law.
- Trust Indenture Act of 1939: Registration of trust indenture documents and supporting data.
- Investment Company Act of 1940: Registration of investment companies.
- Investment Advisers Company Act of 1940: Registration of investment advisers.

---

2. United States, Securities and Exchange Commission, "Regulation S-T." Accessed 15 Sep. 2003 <http://www.sec.gov/about/forms/regs-t.pdf>.

- Sarbanes-Oxley Act of 2002: Requires public-company auditors to register with the PCAOB and adds company registration requirements, including written CEO and CFO certifications of financial statements, a report of management's assessment of internal controls, and other disclosures.

The focus of this chapter is on registration under the 1933 and 1934 Acts and their associated amendments; these are the most common forms of registration involving business people and accountants. (Additional specific procedures for registration under other Acts can be found by reference to the individual Acts.)

In brief, the registration process consists of developing and filing a registration statement with the SEC. A registration statement is generally comprised of two parts, the first part containing information usually included in a prospectus. A prospectus contains information about the company, its history, business, and financial statements. The prospectus, described in more detail later, includes all information to be presented to prospective investors. A copy of the prospectus is customarily submitted in full satisfaction of the requirements of the first part of the registration statement. Other detailed information not included in a prospectus is filed in the second part of the registration statement.

THE SEC'S INTEGRATED DISCLOSURE SYSTEM

Before we discuss and illustrate the registration and reporting processes under the 1933 and 1934 Acts, we first explain the SEC's "integrated disclosure system." This system, implemented in 1983, extensively changed the SEC's emphasis, reporting forms, and disclosure requirements.

Companies registering with the SEC traditionally have had to refer to several sources to determine the requirements, rules, and procedures for reporting to the SEC. For example, Regulation S-X prescribes the form and content of the financial statements. Regulation S-K governs the nonfinancial statement disclosures. Each form specifies the particular items of information required. In addition to Regulation S-X, the financial statement requirements are dealt with in Financial Reporting Releases (FRRs, formerly designated as Accounting Series Releases) as well as in Staff Accounting Bulletins (SABs). The FRRs are used by the SEC to issue new rules, to amend existing rules, and to give its official position on matters relating to financial statements. The SABs give the SEC staff's unofficial interpretations of financial disclosure requirements and explanations of practices the staff is following in administering them.

The problem of knowing which information to present and in what manner is made more complex because the SEC requirements have not necessarily been consistent with generally accepted accounting principles required for external financial reporting. To simplify financial reporting and remove some of the inconsistencies, the SEC adopted its integrated disclosure system in 1983.[3]

The primary objectives of the SEC's integrated disclosure system are:

1. to simplify and improve the quality of disclosures provided to investors and other users of financial information,

2. to reduce the costs involved in the ongoing registration process, and

3. to encourage public companies to create a single set of documents for both shareholder communication and official SEC filings.

The system is based on the belief that a single, comprehensive reporting system, one that integrates the requirements of the 1933 and 1934 Acts, as well as those of shareholders' reports, will improve financial reporting in general and reduce the costs of compliance.

The basic structure of integrated disclosure is found in a Basic Information Package consisting of the following:

*   Audited financial statements
*   Management's Discussion and Analysis
*   Quantitative and Qualitative Disclosures About Market Risk
*   Selected Income and Balance Sheet Data (Selected Financial Data)

The requirements for both the annual report to shareholders and Form 10-K were modified to standardize disclosure items and make them consistent. For example, the annual report to shareholders now must include an expanded management discussion and analysis section, a summary of selected financial data, and an additional year of statements of

3. James Cox, "The Fundamentals of an Electronic-Based Federal Securities Act,"_Washington University Law Quarterly 75 (1997). Accessed 16 Sep. 2003 <http://law.wustl.edu/WULQ/75-2/752-6.html#fnB7>.

income and cash flow statements (with related footnote disclosures). Similarly, Form 10-K was amended (and related modifications were made to Regulation S-K and the proxy rules) by deleting the summary of operations, adding a summary of selected financial data, and requiring a management discussion and analysis of the company's financial condition. In addition, through revisions to Regulation S-X, the requirements for financial statements in annual reports and SEC reports generally are the same.

As part of this integrated disclosure system, several SEC forms were introduced and some old ones deleted. The SEC also reviewed its Accounting Series Releases and rescinded all releases that were no longer applicable. The SEC then started its new series, the FRRs, as mentioned earlier. Specific changes in registration and reporting requirements resulting from the integrated disclosure system will be noted in the sections that follow. (Please also see the two appendices at the end of this chapter, which provide tutorials on finding SEC files online and on the online registration process.)

REGISTRATION AND REPORTING UNDER THE 1933 ACT

To give the reader an idea of the mechanics involved in registration and the review procedures of the SEC, a summary of the process under the 1933 Act is presented. Significant differences between the 1933 and 1934 Acts will be described later in the chapter, but the registration process is similar under these Acts. Keep in mind that the 1933 Act deals with the initial issuance of securities by an issuing public company, while the 1934 Act deals with securities that already exist and that are publicly traded.

Registration Form Selection

Part of the registration process is the selection of the proper form to be used, since the SEC has designed several registration forms for use under each of the Acts. Unlike tax forms, these forms contain no blanks to be filled in. Instead, they have a narrative style, giving general instructions about the items of information to be furnished. Detailed information must be assembled by the companies using the form designated for the type of security being offered as well as the type of company making the offer. Louis H. Rappaport said of this procedure: "The decision as to which form to use for registration in a specific case is usually made by the company in consultation with its counsel. Since the question of which form to use is primarily a legal one, the certifying accountant should not make the decision . . . ."[4]

The decision to raise capital through a public offering of securities must be considered carefully. The benefit of access to the proceeds must be weighed against—among other factors—the costs of registration and reporting to the SEC. Once the decision is made to place a public offering, the initial step is to choose the appropriate registration form. As indicated, this is primarily a legal question. However, business executives, accountants, and underwriters should be familiar with the forms used most frequently. The following sections contain a discussion of the more common registration forms used under the 1933 Act and the procedures for review by the SEC.

Basic Forms

Form S-1 has been the most commonly used form under the 1933 Act, but more than a dozen different forms for various types of companies and special situations are available. Regardless of the form used, certain required information is common to all: (1) nature and history of the issuer's business; (2) capital structure; (3) description of any material contracts, including bonus and profit-sharing arrangements; (4) description of the securities being registered; (5) salaries and security holdings of officers and directors; (6) details of any underwriting arrangements; (7) estimate of the net proceeds and the uses to which such proceeds will be put; and (8) detailed financial information, such as a summary of earnings and certified balance sheets, profit and loss statements, and supporting schedules.[5]

The following list of forms is not comprehensive, but it gives examples of major forms that are used for registration under the 1933 Act. Numerous additional forms of limited, specific use are supplemental to those listed here. A review of the forms will verify the earlier statement that form selection is often a difficult process. The list is in numerical order and is not grouped according to applicability to different industries.

---

4. Louis Rappaport, *SEC Accounting Practice and Procedures*, 3rd ed. (New York: Ronald Press Co., 1972), 8.2.
5. *Securities Regulations* (Englewood Cliffs: Prentice-Hall, 1982), 135.

General Description of Selected 1933 Act Forms[6]

S-1   General form for securities of all issuers for which no other form is prescribed, except that Form S-1 may not be used for registration of securities of foreign governments

S-2   Short form for issuers meeting specified criteria

S-3   Short form for issuers meeting specified criteria and certain transaction requirements

S-4   Form for registration of securities in connection with business combination transactions

S-8   Form for registration of securities to be offered to employees pursuant to certain plans

S-11   Form for registration of securities of certain real estate companies

SB-2   Form for registration of securities to be offered by small businesses

1-A   Form used to notify the SEC of an offering to be made pursuant to Regulation A[7]

The forms listed establish a system of registration, depending on a company's history of public reporting and its prominence in the marketplace. Form S-3 allows for maximum incorporation by reference and is intended for public companies that have a wide following. Incorporation by reference is the ability of a company to *incorporate* the already public information, from periodic reports filed with the SEC or publicly available annual reports, into its registration through *referring* to those previous reports. In general, companies with at least $75 million of voting stock held by nonaffiliates (called the "float" test) and that have filed periodic reports with the SEC for at least twelve months are eligible to use Form S-3. The use of Form S-3 is predicated on the belief that the general public already has significant financial and other information available on companies of a least the size required by the "float test;" thus, the registration disclosures can be less extensive.

Companies qualifying to use Form S-2 are those that have at least a three-year history in reporting to the SEC, but are not as broadly followed as

6. United States, *Code of the Federal Regulations, Title 17-Commodity and Securities Exchanges, Revised as of April 1, 2002* (Washington, D.C.: Government Printing Office, 2002), Part 239.

7. Securities and Exchange Commission, "Form Types Used for Electronic Filing on Edgar," 15 Dec. 2003. Accessed 4 Mar. 2004 <http://www.sec.gov/info/edgar/forms/egdform.htm>.

those companies using Form S-3. Form S-2 provides for incorporation by reference of the 1934 Act reports but also requires disclosure of the basic information package mentioned earlier. This information can be presented in the prospectus itself or by delivering an annual report to shareholders, which contains the basic information, along with the prospectus.

In general, companies that do not qualify to use Form S-2 and S-3 are to use Form S-1. The forms listed beyond S-1, S-2, and S-3 are for special circumstances or industries. For example, Form S-4 is used in registering securities in connection with mergers and related business-combination transactions. S-4 permits incorporation by reference of information from periodic reports already required to be filed under the 1934 Act. Thus, S-1 is used when none of the other 1933 Act forms are applicable. The S-1 requires a complete and comprehensive prospectus without incorporation by reference of material from periodic reports.

In essence, through these different forms the SEC has established a three-tier system for registering securities under the 1933 Act. This system allows for well-established companies, with high-quality corporate reports (including 1934 Act reports) that are widely disseminated in the market, not to provide as much data as companies without such a track record and for which the applicable financial data are not generally available to help investors make decisions. This overview of considerations for form selection is only intended to give the reader an idea of some of the requirement differences between the most common forms. This discussion is far from comprehensive, as each form has an extensive list of eligibility requirements.[8]

The Pre-Filing Conference

The SEC staff is available for pre-filing conferences with companies that have questions about registration. Such conferences often avoid lengthy delays once the registration procedures have begun. The Commission has a long-established policy of having staff available, by conference or correspondence, to advise prospective registrants or their representatives in advance of filing a registration statement. Conferences or correspondence may address the problems confronting a registrant in effecting registration or to resolve specific problems of an unusual nature that are sometimes presented by complicated financial transactions. Experienced practitioners

---

8. Blank SEC forms, which outline eligibility requirements, can be accessed at
<http://www.sec.gov/about/forms/secforms.htm>.

who recognize unique problems regularly follow this procedure and save valuable time for themselves and their clients. The public accountant without experience with SEC filings should consult guidance on the SEC Web site and utilize the pre-filing conference resources if necessary.

A pre-filing conference is usually held with the chief accountant of the division having jurisdiction, but unusual problems have advanced to the Office of the Chief Accountant and even to a hearing with commissioners of the SEC. Most inquiries, however, are resolved at the division level, where firms use this conference privilege to eliminate roadblocks that might otherwise delay registration.

Preparation of the Registration Statement

The need for coordination and cooperation really begins when the registration statement is being prepared for filing. The preparation of a registration statement for filing under the Securities Act of 1933 is almost invariably a combined operation. Representatives of the management of the registering company, the underwriters, the independent public accountants, counsel for the company, counsel for the underwriters, and occasionally, engineers or appraisers all have important roles in preparing the registration document.

Compiling all the information used in registration may well occupy the time of the several people mentioned above for several weeks or months. Additional time is needed to draft the information into a statement acceptable to the company's board of directors.

Anywhere from one-and-a-half to three months may be needed for initial preparation of the statement. This time and effort investment is often necessary to ensure that information is complete and accurate. The accuracy and adequacy of the registration is ultimately the responsibility of the company's officers, underwriters, counsel, and the independent public auditors.

When the initial registration statement is complete, it must be submitted electronically to the SEC in accordance with Regulation S-T. The required filing fee "shall be equal to $92 per $1,000,000 of the maximum aggregate price at which such securities are proposed to be offered."[9]

---

9. United States, *Securities Act of 1933*, Sec. 6.

SEC Review

The review process begins when the SEC receives a completed registration statement from a registrant. The statute provides that the registration statement becomes effective 20 days after it is filed. However, the effective date for the registration may be delayed by the review and amendment procedures or it may be accelerated by action of the registrant.

Select Review Procedures. In late 1980, the SEC implemented major changes in its review procedures in an attempt to reduce delays in the processing of registration statements and periodic SEC reports. The new procedures incorporated a system of "selective review," which allows the SEC to focus its increasingly scarce resources on the highest-priority areas.

All first-time issues continue to receive a thorough review as outlined in the following section. However, repeat offerings by established public companies are reviewed on a selective basis, since they already submit periodic financial reports to the SEC. When the SEC chooses to not review a registration statement, the SEC is relying on its review of the company's recent SEC filings. Regardless of the extent of review by the SEC, the burden of accurate and adequate disclosure ultimately is placed squarely on the shoulders of company management, who must assume liability for what is published in its name. Companies are notified promptly after filing whether their registration statements will be reviewed, and if a company's registration statement will not be reviewed, the registration becomes effective after the 20-day waiting period.

Review of the Statement. A normal examination by the SEC staff consists of a review of the registration statement and a comparison with other information available about the issuer, the industry, and other companies in the industry. This review usually is made by the Division of Corporation Finance. A branch chief gives a copy of the registration statement to an analyst, an attorney, and an accountant. The analyst reviews for proper form and other non-financial information, while the attorney examines the legal aspects, and the accountant reviews the financial statements and schedules. The purpose of this examination, as stated earlier, is to determine compliance with applicable statutes and regulations. The staff of the SEC will try to determine if there is any materially untrue, incomplete, or misleading information in the registration statement; that is, if there is any lack of "full and fair" disclosure. However, this review does not absolve the company or anyone associated with the registration statement from liability under the securities laws.

Memoranda are submitted by each of the three staff experts to the branch chief. A "letter of comments," sometimes known as a "deficiency letter," is then prepared and sent to the company. This letter outlines the deficiencies that the staff has found in the registration statement and makes suggestions for improvements in the document. Excerpts from a comment letter and response to that letter in connection with an S-1 filing are provided in Exhibit 4-2. This exhibit illustrates some comments, suggestions, and additional information requirements that can result from the SEC's review. These items are for illustrative purposes only.

The comments letter, which is not part of the public record, is sent to the registrant as soon as possible so that amendments may be made or other appropriate action may be taken. The letter of comments does not delay the effective date of the registration, but if corrections cannot be made within 20 days, the SEC usually asks the issuer to file a delaying amendment. The submission of any amendment usually renews the 20-day waiting period.

Alternatives Available to SEC for Noncompliance. If a firm does not make an attempt to amend its original document, the SEC has three possible courses of action. The first is to let the statement become effective in a deficient manner, knowing the company will be liable for any actions resulting from misleading information. However, since its goal is to protect the investor, the SEC is generally not willing to let a substantially deficient statement become effective. Furthermore, companies would rather not be the object of lawsuits for their own deficiencies.

The second action the SEC can take is to issue a refusal order. In a refusal order, the SEC must notify an issuer of defects within ten days after the filing date and a hearing must be held sometime during the next ten days to allow for correction. Because of the time pressures and lags involved, this action has been used sparingly by the SEC.

The final course of action is to impose a stop order. A stop order can be issued either before or after the effective date, and it halts further consideration of the statement (if before the effective date) or stops further trading of the security (if after the effective date). As indicated in the following statement from the *Securities Regulations*, such drastic action generally is not needed, since most firms reply quickly to the comments letter.

Exhibit 4-2: Example Correspondence in Connection with an S-1 Filing

```
UNITED STATES
SECURITIES AND EXCHANGE COMMISSION
REGIONAL OFFICE
1375 PEACHTREE STREET N.E., SUITE 700
ATLANTA, GEORGIA 30367

July 1, 2003

Lance Legal, P.A.
Legal & Legal
123 Tort Terrace
Miami, Florida 33128
Re: Isometric, Inc.
File No. 33-98765-A

Dear Mr. Legal:
```

We have the following comments with respect to the Registration Statement on Form S-18 filed in this office on behalf of the above referenced letter on June 8, 2003.

(1) <u>Use of Proceeds</u>, pages 14-15
As required by Instruction 1 to Item 504 of Regulation S-K, please indicate the order of priority of the purposes for which net proceeds will be used.

(2) <u>Management—Directors and Executive Officers</u>, page 30
As required by Item 401(e)(1) of Regulation S-K, please describe Mr. Mercury's position and experience with Monetary Financial Corporation.
As required by Item 401(e)(1) of Regulation S-K, please describe the officer positions held and the nature of the responsibilities undertaken by Mr. Zeus at Olympus Capital Group and Olympus Management.

(3) <u>Principal Shareholders</u>, page 34.
Supplementally, please identify A.B. Ceres and describe his relationship to the registrant or its officers/directors.

(4) <u>Proposed Business—Business Objective</u>, page 23
Your attention is directed to the requirements of Item 2 of Form 8-K which requires the reporting of certain information regarding businesses acquired and Item 7 of that form which sets forth the requirements for the filing of certified financial statements of such companies. The obligations to file such information under Section 13 or 15 of the Exchange Act are in addition to the obligation to include such information in the Prospectus so long as the offering is being made. Thus, if during the offering period, an Issuer determines that material acquisition is probable, a post-effective amendment with audited financial statements of the company to be acquired is required.
Please refer to Release No. 33-6578, which contains the Commission's policies with respect to furnishing certified

financial statements and the resultant consequences where such financial statements are not available.

(5) <u>Item 15—Organization Within Five Years</u>
Please provide the information required by Item 15 regarding transactions between the registrant and Messrs. Legal, Ares and Zeus.

(6) <u>GENERAL COMMENTS</u>
Amendments should be filed in accordance with Rules 470, 471 and 472 of Regulation C. Your attention is directed to Rule 471(a), which requires that one copy be manually signed and that unsigned copies be conformed. Failure to comply with these rules may result in delays in processing and/or review of the amendments.

Please consult Rules 460 and 461 with respect to requests for acceleration of the effective date.

We would appreciate reviewing a written acknowledgment from the Registrant's management that they understand their obligations to file a Report of Sales of Securities and Use of Proceeds thereunder pursuant to Rule 463, and that they intend to discharge the obligation in a timely fashion.

On a supplemental basis, please submit a brief statement by the Underwriter describing (1) the steps taken to verify the information contained in this Registration Statement and; (2) the steps taken to ensure compliance with Rule 15(c)2-8.

If you have any questions concerning these comments please contact the undersigned at 555-555-4768.

> Sincerely,
> Chad Charge, Chief
> Branch of Small Issues

By Betty Barrister,
     Attorney

Todd Templar, Esquire
Templar & Templar
456 Convoluted Circle
Fort Lauderdale, Florida 33316

Morris Mercury, President
Isometric, Inc.
789 Tenth Terrace
South Miami, Florida 33143

National Association of Securities Dealers
1735 K. Street, N.W.
Washington, D.C. 20006
Florida Securities Division

The following is an example of a response to the above letter of comments:

July 11, 2003

U.S. Securities and Exchange Commission
Regional Office
1375 Peachtree Street N.E.
Suite 700
Atlanta, Georgia   30367

Attn: Betty Barrister, Esq.
  Re: Isometric, Inc.—File No. 33-98765-A

Dear Ms. Barrister:
    In connection with your letter of comment dated July 1, 2003 with regard to Isometric, Inc. (the "Company"), I am enclosing herewith the following documents:
    1. Three complete copies of Amendment No. 1 to the Registration Statement on Form S-18, with exhibits, one of which has been manually signed; and
    2. Eight additional copies of Amendment No. 1, five of which have been marked to indicate changes made from the Registration Statement.
    To assist you in your review of this amendment, we set forth below, in the same order as it is set forth in your letter of comment, our response to your letter of comment.

(1) Use of Proceeds, pages 14-15
    Pages 21 and 22 have been amended to address your request. Please note that after paying sales commissions, offering costs and expenses and the consulting fee described in the Registration Statement, the Company will allocate all remaining proceeds as uncommitted working capital. Since this will be the sole purpose for which the net proceeds will be used, the Company is unable to prioritize purpose.

(2) Management—Directors and Executive Officers, page 30
    Based upon our review of Item 401(e)(1) of Regulation S-K, we have amended page 30 to describe Mr. Mercury's position and experience with Gallery Financial Corp. as well as the positions held and the nature of the responsibilities undertaken by Mr. Zeus at Olympus Capital Group and Olympus Management, Inc.

(3) Principal Shareholders, page 34
    A. B. Ceres is the sister of Anne Athena. Mrs. Athena is the President of High Flyer Securities, Inc., the Underwriter of this offering. Ms. Ceres does not reside with Mrs. Athena nor is she financially dependent on her.

(4) <u>Proposed Business—Business Objective</u>, page 23
Your comments concerning the requirements of Items 2
and 7 of Form 8-K and Release No. 33-6578 are duly noted
and will be observed.

(5) <u>Item 15—Organization Within Five Years</u>
Pursuant to your request, we have amended pages 32
and 33 to include the information required by Item 15.

(6) <u>GENERAL COMMENTS</u>
We appreciate your comments and references there
under which have been duly noted and will be observed.
Pursuant to your request, we are enclosing herewith
the written acknowledgement from the Company's
management that they understand their obligations to
file a Report of Sales of Securities and Use of Proceeds
pursuant to Rule 463 promulgated under the Securities
Act of 1933, as amended, and that the Company's
management intends to discharge this obligation in a
timely fashion.
In addition, I am enclosing herewith a brief
statement by High Flyer Securities, Inc., the
Underwriter, describing (1) the steps taken to verify
the information contained in this Registration
Statement; and (2) the steps taken to ensure compliance
with Rule 15c 2-8 of the Securities Exchange Act of
1934, as amended.
To evidence receipt of this filing please stamp the
attached copy of this letter and return same to the
undersigned in the enclosed self-addressed, stamped
envelope provided for your convenience.

Sincerely,
LEGAL AND LEGAL
Lance Legal, P. A.

LCF/ald

cc: Todd, Templar, Esquire
      Mr. Morris Mercury
      Mrs. Anne Athena
      Mr. Zeke Zeus

In effect, because of the weapons outlined above, the SEC has
been able to use the letter of comments to compel correction of the
registration statement. In only rare instances has the SEC had to
resort to the stop order; these have been mainly in cases of flagrant
violations.[10]

---

10. *Securities Regulations, op. cit.*, p. 140, ¶127.4.

The Waiting Period

An important feature in the Securities Act of 1933 is the provision for the 20-day waiting period between the date of filing and the date the registration becomes effective. This process can be accelerated, but with the rapid increase in number of registrations, there has been no "normal" waiting period—the effective date almost always is delayed. In a 2002 GAO report assessing the effects of increased workloads on the SEC, industry officials reported that the normal waiting period is between four to seven weeks,[11] which makes it even more necessary that a statement be adequately prepared.

Indication of Interest. A company need not sit idle during the waiting period; it can move to make an announcement of the prospective issues of securities. This can only be an announcement, however, with no solicitation to buy. The *Securities Regulations* state:

> . . . during the waiting period, dealers may solicit "indications of interest" from their customers, and underwriters may solicit "indications of interest" from dealers. But the dealer cannot enter into contracts of sale, and the underwriters cannot form a selling group of dealers.[12]

An indication of interest expresses possible future intent, but does not obligate an interested party to consummate the transaction. Issuers can obtain indications of interest through oral or written communication through a variety of methods, such as a preliminary or "red herring" prospectus, a "tombstone ad," a radio advertisement, or over the phone.

Word of mouth from an underwriter or dealer to known large investors can prove to be beneficial in stimulating investor interest in a forthcoming security issue. While oral communication may be effective for creating enthusiasm, its effects are probably not as widespread as more systematic advertisement methods.

A preliminary prospectus takes the form of the final prospectus, except that information as to offering price, commissions to dealers, and other matters related to price are omitted. Otherwise, the same investment information must be disclosed. The name "red herring" is derived from the

---

11. United States, General Accounting Office, "SEC Operations: Increased Workload Creates Challenges," Report 02-302. 2002. 17.
12. *Securities Regulations, op. cit.,* p. 137, ¶125.

caption "Preliminary Prospectus" stamped in red ink across the front page, as shown in Exhibit 4-3. A registration statement indicating that the registration has not yet become effective and that the securities may not yet be sold also must be included in print at least as prominent as that in the text of the document.

"Tombstone ads" often are seen in the *Wall Street Journal* and other business periodicals. Section 2(10) of the 1933 Act allows a circular or advertisement that lists sources from which a prospectus may be obtained and by whom orders will be executed. The "tombstone" name comes from the form these advertisements generally take. A typical tombstone ad that might be used before and after a registration statement has become effective is shown in Exhibit 4-4. The tombstone ad is not a selling document, but it is used to locate potential buyers whose interest will be sufficiently aroused to obtain a prospectus and to make additional inquiry about the securities.

Other Waiting Period Activities. During the waiting period, the company also must prepare any substantive amendments or delaying amendments required by the SEC to prevent a deficient statement from becoming effective. Time pressures may become intense as management scrambles to address further requirements detailed in the letter of comments.

Still another matter requires the attention of company management during the waiting period. The 1933 Act requires the managing underwriter to exercise due diligence to help prevent fraud by making careful inquiry into the nature of the security being underwritten. A "due diligence meeting" is called between representatives of the issuer, counsel for the issuer, independent public accountants, underwriters, counsel for the underwriter, and perhaps other professionals. Information is exchanged concerning the registration statement, and final problems are resolved at this meeting.

The Pricing Amendment. When a registration statement is filed, there is general agreement between the issuer and the underwriter as to the type of security being offered and the approximate amount of funds to be raised. However, the final terms relating to any interest or dividend rates, the actual price of the offering, the underwriter's discount or commission, and the net proceeds to the company have not yet been printed on the registration statement. This is accomplished by the "pricing amendment," which is generally filed at about the same time as, or perhaps just after, the "due diligence" meeting.

Exhibit 4-3: An Example of a "Red Herring," or Preliminary Prospectus

> The information in this prospectus is not complete and may be changed. We may not sell these securities until the Securities and Exchange Commission declares our registration statement effective. This prospectus is not an offer to sell these securities and is not soliciting an offer to buy these securities in any state where the offer or sale is not permitted.

Subject to Completion, Dated December 6, 2002
Prospectus

 shares

Common Stock

This is the initial public offering of iPayment, Inc. No public market currently exists for our common stock.

We currently anticipate the initial public offering price of our common stock to be between $_____ and $_____ per share. We have applied to have the shares approved for quotation on the Nasdaq National Market under the symbol "IPMT", subject to notice of issuance.
Investing in the common stock involves risks that are described in the "Risk Factors" section beginning on page 8 of this prospectus.

	Per Share	Total
Public Offering Price	$	$
Underwriting Discount	$	$
Proceeds, before expenses, to iPayment, Inc.	$	$

We have granted the underwriters a 30-day option to purchase up to _____ additional shares to cover any over-allotments.
Delivery of shares will be made on or about _____, 2003.
Neither the Securities and Exchange Commission nor any state securities commission has approved or disapproved of these securities or passed upon the adequacy or accuracy of this prospectus. Any representation to the contrary is a criminal offense.

Source: <http://www.sec.gov/Archives/edgar/data/1140184/000095012302011600/y65042sv1.htm#007>

Exhibit 4-4: An Example of a "Tombstone" Advertisement Used *Before* a Registration Statement Has Become Effective

E*TRADE is pleased to announce that we will have an
allocation of shares to distribute in the upcoming
Be Incorporated initial public offering.

 Be.

Volpe Brown Whelan & Company
Needham & Company, Inc.

IMPORTANT DETAILS:

About Be Incorporated
"We offer the BeOS® operating system, an operating system designed for digital media applications and Internet appliances."

Review the complete preliminary offering prospectus here (PDF).

About the Offering:
Security Type: Common Stock
Offering Size: 6,000,000
Proposed Price Range: $8-10
Proposed Symbol: BEOS

Note: E*TRADE expects to begin accepting indications of interest in this offering in early-mid July.

Be Incorporated has recently filed a securities registration statement with the SEC* announcing its intention to sell shares of common stock in a proposed public stock offering. E*TRADE will have an allocation of shares to distribute to our customers. If you are not yet an E*TRADE customer you can open an account here.

As with all public offerings at E*TRADE, interested customers must complete a brief profile to participate. Here's a sample.

Remember: Check our IPO Bulletin regularly for updates about this offering, including changes to the offering and timing information as it becomes available.

A registration statement for these securities has been filled with the Securities and Exchange Commission but has not yet become effective. These securities may not be sold nor may offers to buy accepted prior to the time the registration statement becomes effective. This communication shall not constitute an offer to sell or the solicitation of an offer to buy nor shall there be any sales of these securities in any jurisdiction in which such offer, solicitation or sale would be unlawful prior to the registration or qualification under the securities laws of such jurisdiction.

"No offer to buy the securities can be accepted and no part of the purchase price can be received until the registration statement becomes effective, and any such offer or indication of interest may be withdrawn and revoked without obligation or commitment of any kind, at any time prior to notice of its acceptance given after the effective date".
*The United States Securities and Exchange Commission

Source: <https://us.etrade.com/e/t/applogic/ IPOTombstone?Message=IPObeost:1>

The pricing amendment changes only the cover page of the prospectus. To illustrate this point, compare Exhibit 4-5, which shows the cover page of a prospectus after the pricing amendment, with Exhibit 4-3, the cover page for the preliminary prospectus. At the time of filing the pricing amendment, the registrant and underwriter usually request acceleration of the effective date of the offering. In some instances, the pricing amendment may be filed after the effective date. Regardless, the effective date generally is within a few days of the pricing amendment.

Effective Registration Statement

Once the deficiencies have been corrected and the SEC staff has informed the Commissioners that they have no significant reservations, the SEC declares the registration statement effective.[13] The issuer and underwriters are then free to proceed with the distribution and sale of the securities.

With certain limited exceptions, all the information compiled as part of the registration statement is public information. Therefore, most information can be accessed and inspected on-line (http://www.sec.gov) or in the Public Reference Room of the SEC in Washington, D.C. Copies of all documents may be obtained, and prospectuses covering recent public offerings may be examined at any SEC office.

Summary of Registration Under the 1933 Act

This brief overview serves to initiate the reader to the registration process required of companies issuing securities to the public in accordance with the 1933 Act. As a summary, Exhibit 4-6 presents a hypothetical example of the registration process. Included in the exhibit is a listing of some of the major events that must take place, the typical participants who are involved, and some idea of the time required for a registration statement to be developed and to become effective. The other securities statutes contain similar registration procedures with variation as to content and purpose.

---

13. As mentioned earlier, the Commission can declare a defective statement effective. However, a company would not knowingly allow that to happen, given the serious legal liability involved.

Exhibit 4-5: An Example of a Prospectus Cover Page After the Pricing Amendment

Filed Pursuant to Rule 424(b)(4)

Registration No. 333-101705

Prospectus

5,000,000 shares

Common Stock

This is the initial public offering of iPayment, Inc. Prior to this offering, there has been no public market for our common stock.

Our shares of common stock have been approved for quotation on the Nasdaq National Market under the symbol "IPMT."

Investing in our common stock involves risks that are described in the "Risk Factors" section beginning on page 8 of this prospectus.

	Per Share	Total
Public Offering Price	$ 16.00	$ 80,000,000
Underwriting Discount	$ 1.12	$ 5,600,000
Proceeds, before expenses, to iPayment, Inc.	$ 14.88	$ 74,400,000

We have granted the underwriters a 30-day option to purchase up to 625,000 additional shares of our common stock to cover any over-allotments.

Delivery of shares of our common stock will be made on or about May 15, 2003.

Neither the Securities and Exchange Commission nor any state securities commission has approved or disapproved of these securities or passed upon the adequacy or accuracy of this prospectus. Any representation to the contrary is a criminal offense.

Source: <http://www.sec.gov/Archives/edgar/data/1140184/000095012303005777/y65042b4e424b4.htm>

Exhibit 4-6:   Illustrative Example of Registration Process

Event	Participants	Agenda	Timetable
Preliminary meeting to discuss issue of new securities	President, VP-Finance, independent accountants, underwriters, counsel	Discuss financial needs; introduce and select type of issue to meet needs.	1 July (Begin)
Form selection	Management, counsel	Select appropriate form for use in registration statement.	3 July (3 days)
Initial meeting of working group	President, VP-Finance, independent accountants, underwriter, counsel for underwriter, company counsel	Assign specific duties to each person in working group; discuss underwriting concerns regarding this issue; discuss accounting concerns regarding the issue.	8 July (8 days)
Second meeting of working group	Same as for initial meeting	Review work assignments; prepare presentation to board of directors.	22 July (22 days)
Meeting of board of directors	Board of directors, members of working group	Approve proposed issue and increase of debt or equity; authorize preparation of materials.	26 July (26 days)
Meeting of company counsel with underwriters	Company counsel, counsel for underwriters, underwriters	Discuss underwriting terms and blue sky concerns.	30 July (30 days)

Event	Participants	Agenda	Timetable
Meeting of working group	Members of working group	Review collected material and examine discrepancies.	6 Aug. (37 days)
Pre-filing conference with SEC staff	Working group members, SEC staff, other experts as needed	Review proposed registration and associated matters of concern: legal, financial, operative.	9 Aug. (40 days)
Additional meetings of working group	Members of working group	Prepare final registration statement and prospectuses.	12-30 Aug. (61 days)
Meeting with board of directors	Board of directors, members of working group	Approve registration statement and prospectuses; discuss related topics and tasks.	6 Sept. (68 days)
Meeting of working group	Members of working group	Draft final corrected registration statement.	10 Sept. (72 days)
Filing registration statement with SEC	Company counsel or representative and SEC staff	File registration statement and pay fee.	12 Sept. (74 days)
Distribution of "red herring" prospectus	Underwriters	Publicize offering.	16 Sept. (78 days)
Receipt of letter of comments	Members of working group	Relate deficiencies in registration statement.	15 Oct. (107 days)

Event	Participants	Agenda	Timetable
Meeting of working group	Members of working group	Correct deficiencies and submit amendments.	21 Oct. (113 days)
"Due diligence" meeting	Management representatives, independent accountants, company counsel, underwriter's counsel, underwriters, other professionals as needed	Exchange final information and discuss pertinent problems relating to underwriting and issue.	24 Oct. (116 days)
Pricing amendment	Management, underwriters	Add the amounts for the actual price, underwriter's discount or commission, and net proceeds to company to the amended registration statement.	25 Oct. (117 days)
Notice of acceptance	SEC staff	Report from SEC staff on acceptance status of price-amended registration statement.	28 Oct. (120 days)
Statement becomes effective			30 Oct. (122 days)

REGISTRATION AND REPORTING UNDER THE 1934 ACT

The Securities Exchange Act of 1934 requires the registration of the many participants in the securities market. The 1934 Act is much broader in scope than the 1933 Act. Whereas the 1933 Act applies only to the initial issuance of securities, the 1934 Act applies to most large and some smaller companies, stock exchanges, brokers and dealers, and national securities associations. In addition, the 1934 Act specifically prohibits manipulative devices, includes provisions for insider trading, proxy solicitations, and tender offers, and provides for "margin" requirements. The specific types of companies and the sections of the 1934 Act under which they must report periodically to the SEC include the following:

- Companies whose securities are listed on the national securities exchanges [Sections 12(a) and (b)];
- Companies whose securities are traded over the counter, if those companies have total assets of $10 million and 500 or more stockholders [Section 12(g)];
- Companies with over 300 stockholders of a class of securities that are registered under the 1933 Act [Section 15(d)]. Even with fewer than 300 stockholders, there may be a reporting obligation in the fiscal year that a 1933 Act filing becomes effective.

The breadth of coverage of the 1934 Act can be illustrated by considering the 1934 Act report forms.

Report Forms

Since registration and reporting requirements under the 1934 Act are very broad in coverage, there are 12 separate categories of report forms:[14]

- Forms for registration of national securities exchanges
- Forms for reports to be filed by officers, directors, and security holders
- Forms for registration of securities on national securities exchanges
- Forms for annual and other reports of issuers
- Forms for statements made in connection with exempt tender offers
- Forms for registration of brokers and dealers on over-the-counter markets

---

14. *Code of the Federal Regulations, Title 17—Commodity and Securities Exchanges, op. cit.,* Part 249.

- Forms for reports by certain exchange members, brokers, and dealers
- Forms for reports concerning stabilization
- Forms for registration and reporting by national securities associations and affiliates
- Forms for registration of securities information processors
- Forms for registration of municipal securities dealers
- Forms for reporting missing, lost, stolen, or counterfeit securities

Selection of Forms

As with registration under the 1933 Act, responsibility for selection of the appropriate forms to be used rests with the registrant and its legal counsel. To illustrate the numerous forms, a brief description of some of the basic 1934 Act forms is given below, along with a list of the schedules of supporting information that must be filed. The numerical forms are for registration, while the numerical-alphabetical forms are for the periodic reports associated with such prior registration – e.g., a firm registering by using Form 10 would use Form 10-K for its annual reports thereafter.

Selected Forms – 1934 Act

8-A	Short form for registration of certain classes of securities
10	General form for registration of securities for which no other form is specified
BD	General registration form for brokers and dealers on over-the-counter markets
6-K	Current report for a foreign issuer
8-K	Current report required to be filed after the occurrence of a "material" event
10-K	Annual report for which no other form is prescribed
11-K	Annual reports for employee stock purchase or similar plans

10-Q	Quarterly reports containing specified information filed for each of the first three quarters of a company's fiscal year
20-F[15]	Annual report of foreign private issuers
40-F	Annual report of certain Canadian issuers

Supporting Schedules—1934 Act

Article 5—Commercial and Industrial Companies	
Schedule I	Condensed financial information of registrant
Schedule II	Valuation and qualifying accounts
Schedule III	Real estate and accumulated depreciation
Schedule IV	Mortgage loans on real estate
Schedule V	Supplemental information concerning property-casualty, insurance operations

Article 6—Registered Investment Companies

Management Investment Companies	
Schedule I	Investments in securities of unaffiliated issuers
Schedule II	Investment other than securities
Schedule III	Investments in and advances to affiliates
Schedule IV	Investments - securities sold short
Schedule V	Open option contracts written
Unit Investment Trusts	
Schedule I	Investment in securities
Schedule II	Allocation of trust assets to series of trust shares
Schedule III	Allocation of trust income and distributable funds to series of trust shares

---

15. Form 20-F is used by foreign private issuers as an initial registration statement and as an annual report under the Exchange Act of 1934. The SEC revised substantially the form of disclosures allowed in Release No. 33-7745 (International Series Release No. 1205), where the SEC accepted the International Organization of Securities Commissions' integrated disclosure standards for foreign issuers. This revision of the disclosure format of the 20-F is progress toward international harmonization of financial reporting standards. Example 20-F's can be accessed through the SEC's online database EDGAR (see Appendix 1 at the end of Chapter 4 for EDGAR access assistance).

Face amount certificate investment companies	
Schedule I	Investment in securities of unaffiliated issuers
Schedule II	Investments in and advances to affiliates and income thereon
Schedule III	Mortgage loans on real estate and interest earned on mortgages
Schedule IV	Qualified assets on deposit
Schedule V	Amounts due from officers and directors
Schedule VI	Certificate reserves
Schedule VII	Valuation and qualifying accounts

Article 6A—Employee Stock Purchase, Savings and Similar Plans

Schedule I	Investments
Schedule II	Allocation of plan assets and liabilities to investment program
Schedule III	Allocation of plan income and changes in plan equity to investment programs

Article 7—Insurance Companies

Schedule I	Summary of investments—other than investments in related parties
Schedule II	Condensed financial information of registrant
Schedule III	Supplementary insurance information
Schedule IV	Reinsurance
Schedule V	Valuation and qualifying accounts
Schedule VI	Supplemental information concerning property-casualty insurance operations

Review of 1934 Act Registrations

While substantially all initial registration forms under the 1933 Act receive a full review, only a portion of 1934 Act registrations receive a full review. The GAO reported that from 1991 to 2000, the portion of all corporate filings receiving a full review, a full financial review, or a review of selected disclosures decreased from 21 percent to 8 percent.[16] SEC staff screen all 1934 Act registrations and determine if the registration should receive 1) a full review, 2) a lesser degree of monitoring, or 3) no review. This screening

16. United States, General Accounting Office, *op.cit.,* p. 22.

decision is based on several factors including the financial condition of the registrant and whether the registrant has been recently investigated by the SEC's Division of Enforcement. The review process for a full review of 1934 Act registrations is similar to those of the 1933 Act, in that an analyst, attorney and accountant review the registration, and the results of any deficiencies are communicated to the registrant via a letter of comments. The Division of Corporate Finance can turn over any registrant who is unresponsive to issues unveiled in the letter of comments to the Division of Enforcement.[17]

Differences Between Registration Under the 1933 and 1934 Acts

There are several differences in the registration procedures and reporting requirements under the 1933 and 1934 Acts. The scope of the registration itself is the first such difference. The 1933 Act requires registration for all initial offerings of securities for public sale. Thus, to raise money in the primary capital market essentially requires 1933 Act registration, and a prospectus always is required. Under the 1933 Act, registration is for a specific security to be issued in a specific amount. The SEC requires a post-effective report on the sale of a new security to verify the amount sold and to cancel any excess not sold. Under the 1934 Act, however, an entire class of securities is registered with no amount specified. The registration covers the amount of securities outstanding and any additional shares of the class of security that have been previously issued but are currently held by the company (treasury stock). Thus, the 1934 Act deals with the secondary capital markets that trade existing securities; no prospectus is required.

Another difference between the Acts is the extensive reporting requirements of the 1934 Act. Since securities listed under the 1934 Act are traded continuously over many years, the statute provides for regular disclosure of company activities through annual, quarterly, and special reports. The most widely used forms are the 8-K for significant current events, the 10-K for annual reports, and the 10-Q for quarterly reports (The general content of these reports is described in Chapter 5).

The extensive reporting requirements of the 1934 Act are not confined to the periodic reports mentioned above. Insider trading requirements, proxy solicitation rules, and regulation of tender offers are but a few additional examples of the broad reporting provisions of the 1934 Act.

---

17. United States. General Accounting Office, "Securities Regulation: Background and Selected Statistics on the SEC's Full Disclosure Program," Report GGD-86-87FS, 1986,. p. 11–13.

Additional amendments that have modified this Act include those incorporated in the Foreign Corrupt Practices Act of 1977 and portions of the Sarbanes-Oxley Act, which were both discussed in Chapter 3.

REGISTRATION UNDER OTHER ACTS

Registration requirements are similar for the other Acts supervised and enforced by the SEC. Registrations are reviewed for compliance with the specific statutes, and for completeness and fairness of disclosure. Periodic reports are required by every Act except the 1933 Act and the Trust Indenture Act of 1939. The periodic reports contain the same basic information, and practically all this information is made public. Specific questions about the unique aspects of each Act can be answered by consulting the text of the Act itself.

SUMMARY

Corporations register securities with the SEC to tap funding available via public capital markets. Successful registration of securities with the SEC involves a number of complicated tasks and requires the dedication of company executives and coordination of the activities of several experts such as underwriters, attorneys, and public accountants. The process is a costly one.

The goal and responsibility of the SEC is to protect investors by requiring full disclosure of an issuer's activities so that investors can reach informed decisions. This objective is obviously not always achieved, but an integrated, cooperative system is encouraged by the registration and reporting processes described in this chapter.

DISCUSSION QUESTIONS

1. What is the overall purpose of the SEC registration and review process?

2. Briefly outline the registration process for the 1933 Act.

3. What information is commonly required in the basic registration forms?

4. Briefly describe the review procedure followed by the SEC staff upon receipt of a registration statement.

5. What is the purpose of the letter of comments?

6. If a registration statement is deficient, what actions may the SEC take? What are the results of these actions?

7. Why has the SEC instituted a system of "selective review"?

8. While waiting for completion of the review, what can a company do in anticipation of approval from the SEC to proceed?

9. What is a "red herring," or preliminary prospectus? What information does it contain?

10. How do underwriters exercise due diligence under the 1933 Act?

11. Once a company becomes registered under the 1934 Act, to what major regulatory provisions is it subject?

12. What is a proxy?

13. What are the primary differences between the requirements for registration under the 1933 and the 1934 Acts?

APPENDIX 1: USING EDGAR TO ACCESS COMPANY FILINGS

EDGAR stands for "Electronic Data Gathering, Analysis, and Retrieval system." This system is owned and operated by the SEC, and it is the system public companies use to electronically file their 10-Ks, 10-Qs, and other forms with the SEC. Beginning May 6, 1996, all domestic public companies were required to use EDGAR to make their filings. In 2002, the SEC proposed a new rule mandating the use of EDGAR by foreign private issuers and foreign governments for their securities documents, including registration statements under the Securities Act of 1933 and registration statements, reports, and other documents under the Securities Exchange Act of 1934.

The SEC makes company filings available free of charge through the Internet on its Web site at http://www.sec.gov. This Web site has many different links; however, the section where filings can be found is "Filings & Forms (EDGAR)." This link is shown below:

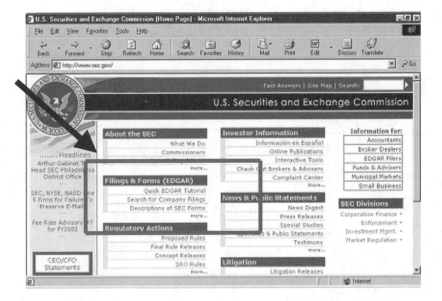

After clicking on the link "Search for Company Filings" under the "Filings & Forms (EDGAR)" section, the user is brought to the following screen:

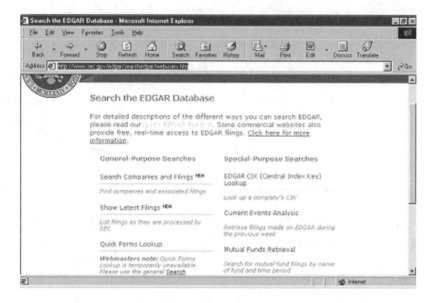

The "Show Latest Filings" link shows most recent filings the EDGAR system has received from any type of SEC filer, including individuals and companies, paper filers, and electronic filers. This link is similar to the "Current Events Analysis" link, which allows the retrieval of filings made during the previous week. When one wants to look at a specific company's documents, however, "Search Companies and Filings" is the link to choose. Clicking "Search Companies and Filings" enables the user to search for filings by entering either the company's name or Central Index Key (CIK). For example, if the user wanted access to Nike filings, then "Nike" would be entered under "Company name."

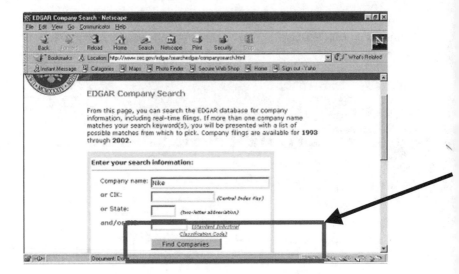

After entering the company name, clicking the "Find Companies" button brings up a screen showing all companies in the EDGAR database with that name. In this case, the system displays two companies, Nike Inc. and Nike Securities LP.

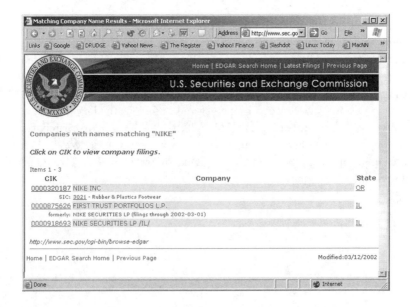

Clicking "Nike Inc" brings up the following screen:

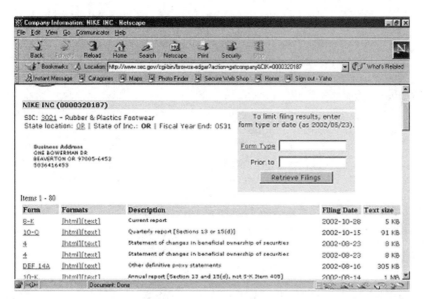

This screen shows all filings made by Nike beginning with the most recent and descending in reverse-chronological order. Narrowing the list of forms is accomplished by inputting "10-K" in "Form Type" field, in which only Nike's 10-Ks are displayed. The box "Prior to" also limits the results to a certain range of time.

Using EDGAR on the SEC's Web site to find company filings has three benefits: it is relatively easy to use, takes minimal time, and is free of charge.

APPENDIX 2: SUBMITTING SEC FILINGS THROUGH EDGAR

This section outlines the typical steps companies take to electronically file reports with the SEC using the Electronic Data Gathering, Analysis, and Retrieval system (EDGAR). EDGAR is intended to benefit electronic filers, enhance the speed and efficiency of SEC processing, and make corporate and financial information available to investors, the financial community, and others in a matter of minutes.

In early 1993, the Commission began to mandate electronic filings through EDGAR, and on May 30, 2000, EDGAR began accepting filings via the Internet. More detailed information regarding filing using EDGAR can be found in the EDGAR Filing Manual, which can be obtained from the SEC's Web site at http://www.sec.gov/info/edgar/filermanual.htm. This section merely presents an overview of the EDGAR filing process.

PREPARING TO FILE THROUGH EDGAR

Before becoming an EDGAR filer, a company must complete the following five steps:

1. Fax a Form ID application to the SEC to get access codes

    Before using the EDGAR system, a company must file an application to register as an EDGAR filer—a company cannot access the EDGAR Web site without certain codes. After the SEC processes the application, the company receives four access codes: the Central Index Key (CIK), the CIK Confirmation Code (CCC), the password, and the Password Modification Authorization Code (PMAC). The CIK is a number that uniquely identifies each filer, and it helps the SEC distinguish between filers with similar names. The CCC accompanies the CIK in the header of filings to show the filings are properly authorized. The password allows companies to log onto the EDGAR system, submit filings, and change their CCC. The CIK is public and a company may give it and the CCC to its agent to make submissions on its behalf, but companies should hold their password in strictest confidence. Companies use the

PMAC4 to authorize a change of password. It is a very private code, and only one or two people in an organization should know this code. Once a company has obtained all these access codes, it is able to login to EDGAR, download submission templates, transmit submissions, run company queries, update company information, and change its password/CCC.

2. Obtain EDGAR-compatible hardware (computer equipment) and software

Companies need certain hardware and software to transmit submissions to EDGAR. Recommended minimum requirements are a moving target, but they currently include the following: an IBM or compatible PC with a Pentium II 250 + MHz, Windows '95 or better, 64 MB of RAM, 70 MB hard drive space to install the software and 10 to 20 MB for submission preparation and transfer; monitor; printer; Internet browser, such as Netscape Navigator version 4.0 or higher or Internet Explorer version 5.0 or higher; and Internet access or direct dial access.

3. Secure an ISP for access to the Internet, or configure its Windows operating system and modem for direct dial (PPP)

4. Download EDGARLink software and templates from EDGAR Web site

EDGARLink helps companies prepare, submit, and correct submissions by formatting information in the format required for a submission in EDGAR. EDGARLink also checks for formatting errors in documents and submissions prior to transmitting which reduces the chance of filing suspense. EDGARLink also assists in troubleshooting errors and compresses the filing to reduce storage space and transmission time. Submission templates consist of sets of fields and information that companies need to fill out for specific submission types, like 10-Ks, 10-Qs, etc. Once a company has its access codes, it can login to the EDGAR Web site at http://www.edgarfiling.sec.gov and download EDGARLink and the necessary templates.

5.   Install EDGARLink software

Once a company downloads and installs EDGARLink, it can download and install the submission templates for the particular form it is filing. After completing the appropriate template(s), companies are ready to transmit their submissions to the SEC via EDGAR.

Transmitting filings via EDGAR

After obtaining the necessary access codes, hardware, and software, as well as preparing the filing itself, a company is ready to transmit documents through the EDGAR system. The first step in submitting filings is to log on to the EDGAR Web site at http://www.edgarfiling.sec.gov. After logging into EDGAR with the access codes, the following option menu appears on the left-hand side of the browser window as shown below:

Under the Downloads section of the option menu, companies can download the EDGARLink software and submission templates. To transmit a filing, however, the user needs to click on the link "Transmit" under the Information Exchange section. The following Transmit Submission page appears:

The user should next click on the [Browse...] button, which opens the Upload File window.

The next step is to find the submission and to click on the open button. After the file name of the transmission appears in the "Submission File Name" box, the user should click the "Transmit LIVE Filing" button. Once this button is clicked, EDGAR will process the submission. After transmitting a submission, filers may also check on the EDGAR Web site to ensure the SEC received and accepted the submission.

5

A Breakdown of
SEC Reports

In Chapter 4 we examined the registration process and identified the forms used in that process. An appreciation for the extremely heavy workload of corporations and the SEC divisions in complying with the requirements of the various Securities and Exchange Acts can be gained by multiplying by several thousand each year the procedures described. Besides handling numerous first-time Securities Act registration statements, the SEC also receives quarterly, annual, and special reports from thousands of U.S. firms.

In Chapter 5 we outline and illustrate the most common forms required for registration and reporting.

OVERVIEW

Of the numerous forms available for reporting to the SEC (see Chapter 4), only the most commonly used forms will be discussed here. Excerpts from reports were captured from the SEC archives and can be accessed online. Due to the lengthy nature of these reports, each report is displayed through its first page only. Internet URL references directly follow so that interested readers can access full copies of the reports. These reports are based on actual company filings and serve as useful examples of corporate reporting. Because of continuous changes in reporting standards (established by the FASB, the SEC, and other regulatory agencies), the content of the printed examples may not completely reflect current requirements. However, the general approach is indicative of the type of disclosure presented in SEC reports.

The forms sent to the SEC are mostly narrative reports accompanied by financial statements and schedules. Company executives are responsible for the preparation of the reports, and independent public accountants attest to the financial statements. Each form used in reporting to the SEC has varying requirements as to financial data. The most common forms are:

- Form S-1, used for many registrations pursuant to the 1933 Act,
- Form 10-K, the primary form for yearly reports under the 1934 Act,
- Form 10-Q, used by firms to report quarterly operations under the 1934 Act,
- Form 8-K, used by firms to report any significant current event affecting the company, and
- Proxy statements, used in conjunction with proxy solicitations for the periodic meetings of stockholders.

REGISTRATION UNDER THE 1933 ACT

Traditionally, Form S-1 has been the most commonly used form for firms registering securities to be sold in the primary capital markets. As explained in Chapter 4, Forms S-1, S-2, and S-3 form a basic three-tier framework for registering securities under the 1933 Act, depending on the qualifications of the registering firm. Form S-1 will be illustrated, since it requires the most extensive disclosures.

Form S-1 is generally comprised of the following components:

1. Facing sheet, which is the outside cover or cover page for the filing.

2. Cross-reference sheet, which shows the page location in the prospectus of items 1-12 prescribed by Form S-1.

3. Part I—the prospectus, which is the material generally distributed as a separate booklet to prospective purchasers of securities. The prospectus contains information and financial statements as specified by items 1 through 12 of Form S-1. The prospectus also must contain any additional data needed to make it meaningful and not misleading.

4. Part II, which contains additional information that is submitted as required by items 13-17 of Form S-1 and other rules and regulations of the SEC. For example, included in Part II are the signatures of company officers and directors, the consent of counsel and other experts (such as accountants), and the financial schedules required by Section 12 of Regulation S-X.

A general description of the items required in Parts I and II of Form S-1 is given in Exhibit 5-1. Not all items will appear in every registration statement. Also, some information may be incorporated by reference to another statement being filed with the SEC and need not be duplicated in the Form S-1 filing.

A copy of a complete registration statement would be needed to explain the entire Form S-1. However, an examination of several items will appropriately illustrate the narrative and tabular nature of the form.

Using a sample Form S-1 filing for a company named iPayment, Inc., Exhibits 5-2 through 5-8 show portions of the actual filings from the SEC's Web site to demonstrate the information provided.

The first part of the S-1 filing presented is the prospectus summary (item 3) in Exhibit 5-2. The prospectus summary serves as an introduction to the filing and provides a summary of the offering, the company, and selected financial information.

Exhibit 5-1: Items Required in Parts I and II of Form S-1

Part I

1. Forepart of the Registration Statement and Outside Front Cover Page of Prospectus
2. Inside Front and Outside Back Cover Pages of Prospectus
3. Summary Information, Risk Factors, and Ratio of Earnings to Fixed Charges
4. Use of Proceeds
5. Determination of Offering Price
6. Dilution
7. Selling Security Holders
8. Plan of Distribution
9. Description of Securities to Be Registered
10. Interest of Named Experts and Counsel
11. Information with Respect to the Registrant (including such items as description of business, property, legal proceedings, financial statements, supplements, financial information, management's discussion and analysis, changes in accountants and executive compensation.)
12. Disclosure of Commission Position on Indemnification for Securities Act Liabilities

Part II

13. Other Expenses of Issuance of Distribution
14. Indemnification of Directors and Officers
15. Recent Sales of Unregistered Securities
16. Exhibits and Financial Statement Schedules
17. Undertakings[a]

Source: http://www.sec.gov/about/forms/forms-1.pdf

---

[a] Part II of Form S-1 requires additional backup information, which will not be illustrated here, but can be accessed at http://www.sec.gov/Archives/edgar/data/1140184/000095012302011600/y65042sv1.htm#022.

Exhibit 5-2: Prospectus Summary

This summary highlights information contained elsewhere in this prospectus, but does not contain all the information that is important to you. You should read this entire prospectus carefully, including the section entitled "Risk Factors," our consolidated financial statements and the related notes included elsewhere in this prospectus, before making an investment decision. In this prospectus, we define a merchant as "active" if the merchant processes at least one credit or debit transaction in a given month. Unless otherwise specified or the context otherwise requires, references in this prospectus to "we," "our" and "us" refer to iPayment, Inc. and its direct and indirect subsidiaries on a consolidated basis.

Our Business

We are a leading provider of credit and debit card-based payment processing services to small merchants. As of September 30, 2002, we provided our services to approximately 50,000 active small merchants located across the United States. The small merchants we serve typically generate less than $250,000 of charge volume per year and have an average transaction value of approximately $80. These merchants have traditionally been underserved by larger payment processors due to the difficulty in identifying, servicing and managing the risks associated with these merchants. As a result, these merchants have historically paid higher transaction fees than larger merchants.

Our payment processing services enable merchants to process both traditional card-present, or "swipe," transactions, as well as card-not-present transactions. A card-not-present transaction occurs whenever a customer does not physically present a payment card at the point-of-sale and may occur over the Internet or by mail, fax or telephone. Our processing services include card authorization, data capture, settlement, merchant accounting, risk management, fraud detection, merchant assistance and support and chargeback services. By outsourcing card authorization, data capture, settlement and merchant accounting to third parties, we maintain a scalable, efficient operating structure.

We believe our experience and knowledge in providing payment processing services to small merchants gives us the ability to effectively identify, evaluate and manage the payment processing needs and risks that are unique to small businesses.

We market and sell our services primarily through our relationships with over 500 independent sales organizations, or ISOs, which act as an external sales force in communities throughout the United States. By providing the same high level of service and support to our ISOs as we do to our merchant customers, we maintain our access to an experienced sales force of approximately 2,000 sales professionals who will market our services, with minimal direct investment in sales infrastructure and management. After an ISO refers a merchant to us and we execute a processing agreement with that merchant, we pay the referring ISO a percentage of the revenues generated by that merchant. Although our relationships with ISOs are non-exclusive, we believe that our understanding of the unique payment processing needs of small merchants enables us to develop compelling incentives for ISOs to continue to refer newly identified merchants to us. We also maintain an open dialogue with our ISOs, allowing us to quickly address their concerns and any problems facing the merchants they refer to us.

THE OFFERING

Common stock offered	shares
Common stock outstanding after this offering	shares
Use of proceeds	We intend to use the estimated net proceeds from this offering as follows: • $51.0 million to repay outstanding indebtedness; and • $ million for general corporate purposes, including working capital and potential acquisitions.
Proposed Nasdaq National Market symbol	"IPMT"
Risk factors	See "Risk Factors" for a discussion of factors you should carefully consider before deciding to invest in shares of our common stock.

The total number of outstanding shares of common stock above excludes:
- 1,994,873 shares of common stock issuable upon exercise of outstanding stock options as of November 15, 2002 at a weighed average exercise price of $2.64 per share;
- 4,350,600 shares of common stock issuable upon exercise of outstanding warrants as of November 15, 2002 at a weighted average exercise price of $0.01 per share; and
- the conversion of $16.9 million of our outstanding convertible subordinated promissory notes into 1,576,154 shares of common stock assuming conversion on December 1, 2002.

Except as otherwise indicated, information in this prospectus:
- assumes the underwriters have not exercised their option to purchase shares to cover over-allotments;
- gives effect to a for split of our outstanding common stock immediately prior to this offering; and
- reflects the conversion of 2,577,200 shares of our outstanding mandatorily redeemable convertible preferred stock into the same number of shares of common stock upon completion of this offering.

	Year Ended December 31,			Nine Months Ended September 30,	
	1999	2000	2001	2001 (unaudited)	2002
	(in thousands, except share and per share data and charge volume)				
Statement of Operations Data:					
Revenues	$ 27,856	$ 20,705	$ 38,889	$ 23,634	$67,268
Operating expenses:					
Costs of services	22,068	19,028	33,633	18,447	54,734
Selling, general and administrative	4,215	6,586	3,782	2,373	4,488
Depreciation and amortization	606	2,828	4,299	3,011	3,759
Restructuring costs	—	1,585	(131)	—	—
Total operating expenses	26,889	30,027	41,583	23,831	62,981
Income (loss) from operations	967	(9,322)	(2,694)	(197)	4,287
Other income (expense):					
Interest income (expense), net	197	(815)	(2,928)	(1,564)	(3,914)
Other	(796)	(412)	625	631	(1)
Total other expense	(599)	(1,227)	(2,303)	(933)	(3,915)
Income (loss) before income taxes	368	(10,549)	(4,997)	(1,130)	372
Income tax provision (benefit)	84	2	(107)	3	466
Net income (loss)	284	(10,551)	(4,890)	(1,133)	(94)
Preferred stock accretion	—	—	(874)	(550)	(1,096)
Net income (loss) available to common stockholders	$284	$(10,551)	$(5,764)	$(1,683)	$(1,190)
Basic and diluted earnings (loss) per common share:					
Earnings (loss) per share	$6.15	$(15.90)	$(0.6.	$(0.20)	$(0.12)
Weighted average shares outstanding	46,148	663,682	8,862,727	8,589,240	10,286,888
Financial and Other Data:					
EBITDA(1)	$1,573	$(6,494)	$1,605	$2,814	$8,046
Charge volume (in millions)	$367	$310	$802	$459	$1,507

	Actual(2)	September 30, 2002 Pro Forma Adjustments	Total Pro Forma	Pro Forma As Adjusted
		(numbers in thousands)		
Balance Sheet Data:				
Cash and cash equivalents	$1,387	$ —	$ 1,387	$
Total assets	110,252	—	110,252	
Long-term debt, net of current portion and discount	59,797	12,606 (3)	72,403	
Mandatorily redeemable convertible preferred stock	6,250	(6,250) (4)	—	
Total stockholders' equity	$8,654	$ 6,250 (4)	$ 14,904	$

(1) EBITDA is defined as earnings from operations before interest income and expense, income taxes, depreciation and amortization. EBITDA is presented supplementally because management believes it allowed for a more complete analysis of results of our operations. This information should not be considered as an alternative to any measure of performance or liquidity as promulgated under accounting principles generally accepted in the United States, such as net income or cash provided by or used in operating, investing or financing activities, nor should it be considered as an indicator of our overall financial performance. Our calculation of EBITDA may be different from the calculation used by other companies and, therefore, comparability may be limited.

(2) The unaudited pro forma balance sheet data has been derived from our audited balance sheet as of September 30, 2002, included elsewhere in this prospectus.

(3) Represents the issuance of $16.8 million, net of discount of $4.2 million, of subordinated promissory notes and warrants to purchase 1,174,250 shares of common stock subsequent to September 30, 2002.

(4) Represents the conversion of 2,577,200 shares of our mandatorily redeemable convertible preferred stock into common stock.

Exhibit 5-3 illustrates how iPayment, Inc. proposed to use the proceeds of the offering and provides an example of the frequent use of narrative to supplement numerical information.

Exhibit 5-3: Use of Proceeds

We estimate that we will receive approximately $ million in net proceeds from the sale of our common stock in this offering, or approximately $ million if the underwriters' over-allotment option is exercised in full, based on an assumed initial offering price of $ per share and after deducting the estimated underwriting discounts and commissions and estimated offering expenses payable by us.

We currently intend to use the estimated net proceeds from this offering as follows:

- $51.0 million for the repayment of outstanding subordinated promissory notes; and
- $ million of the net proceeds for general corporate purposes, including working capital and the acquisition of businesses and merchant portfolios that are complementary to our own. Currently, we have no specific plans or commitments with respect to any acquisition. We cannot assure you that we will complete any acquisitions or that, if completed, any acquisition will be successful.

As of September 30, 2002, we had notes outstanding in an aggregate principal amount of $69.5 million, owed to various individuals and entities, with interest rates ranging from 0% to 14% as described below. Subsequent to September 30, 2002, we have issued an additional $16.8 million of subordinated promissory notes. We will repay the following notes with the proceeds from this offering:

Aggregate Principal Amount of Subordinated Promissory Notes	Maturity Date	Interest Rate
$2,581,701	August 31, 2003	12.00%
$1,020,292	December 31, 2003	10.00%
$9,925,000	January 1, 2004	12.00%
$2,800,000	March 1, 2004	4.75%
$15,775,000	April 1, 2004	12.00%
$7,500,000	May 30, 2004	12.00%
$1,100,000	May 30, 2004	14.00%
$4,000,000	April 11, 2006	14.00%
$5,000,000	August 31, 2007	6.00%
$1,316,105	August 22, 2007	12.00%

Of these notes, $ million were issued within a year of the date of this prospectus. In each case, we used the proceeds to fund acquisitions of businesses and portfolios of merchant accounts, as well as to fund working capital. In addition, $11.4 million of the notes to be repaid are held by affiliates and related parties. Please see "Certain Relationships and Related Transactions."

We will retain broad discretion in the allocation and use of the remaining net proceeds of this offering. Pending application of the net proceeds, as described above, we will invest any remaining proceeds in short-term, investment-grade, interest-bearing securities.

Source: http://www.sec.gov/Archives/edgar/data/1140184/000095012302011600/y65042sv1.htm

Exhibit 5-4: Management's Discussion and Analysis of Financial Condition and Results of Operations

The following discussion and analysis of our financial condition and results of operations should be read in conjunction with "Selected Historical Consolidated Financial Information and Other Data" and our consolidated financial statements and related notes included elsewhere in this prospectus.

Overview

We are a leading provider of credit and debit card-based payment processing services to small merchants. As of September 30, 2002, we provided our services to approximately 50,000 active small merchants located across the United States. Our payment processing services enable our merchants to process both traditional card-present, or swipe transactions, as well as card-not-present transactions. A traditional card-present transaction, occurs whenever a cardholder physically presents a credit or debit card to a merchant at the point-of-sale. Card-not-present transactions occur whenever the customer does not physically present a payment card at the point-of-sale and may occur over the Internet or by mail, fax or telephone.

Our predecessor, iPayment Technologies, Inc., was formed in 1992 as a California corporation. In July 2000, iPayment Technologies purchased assets from two former affiliates in exchange for the assumption of debt, $400,000 in cash, a $2.0 million note and the issuance of 5,000 shares of iPayment Technologies' common stock. We refer to this as our reorganization. We accounted for our reorganization as a purchase with the majority stockholders allocating their investment to the fair value of assets acquired and liabilities assumed and the excess basis allocated to goodwill. The reorganization was affected in order to transfer ownership of certain assets owned by former affiliates of iPayment Technologies, and to separate iPayment Technologies from its former affiliates. Also in connection with our reorganization, Caymas, LLC purchased a majority interest in iPayment Technologies.

In December 2000, iPayment Technologies implemented a restructuring plan, which resulted in a reduction in overhead costs and personnel. Expenses related to the restructuring included severance and future lease costs, write downs of fixed assets and leasehold improvements.

In February 2001, we were formed by the majority stockholders of iPayment Technologies under the name iPayment Holdings, Inc. as a holding company for iPayment Technologies and other card processing businesses. We then appointed Gregory Daily as our Chief Executive Officer and Chairman of the Board. In April 2001, we acquired a 94.63% interest in iPayment Technologies, and in July 2002, we acquired the remaining outstanding shares of iPayment Technologies, which then became our wholly owned subsidiary, in each case by issuing our shares to iPayment Technologies stockholders in exchange for iPayment Technologies shares.

In August 2002, we were reincorporated in Delaware under the name iPayment, Inc.

Source: <http://www.sec.gov/Archives/edgar/data/1140184/000095012302011600/y65042sv1.htm>

Management's discussion and analysis of selected financial data is a very important element of item 11, information with respect to the registrant. The information to be included is required by Regulation S-K. Summarized income statement and balance sheet data must be presented for each of the last three years and any additional periods to keep the summary from being misleading. Management's discussion and analysis must address the company's financial condition and results of operations, including specific information on liquidity, capital resources, and any material events or uncertainties known to management that would cause the reported information not to be indicative of the company's future operating results or financial condition. An example of such disclosure (showing only part of the information) is provided as Exhibit 5-4.

Another major portion of the information with respect to the registrant is the description of business (item 11). iPayment describes its business of providing merchant transaction processing for small companies, as shown in Exhibit 5-5.

Portions of the narrative have been provided to illustrate the wide variety of subjects covered. The financial statements included in Form S-1 are prescribed by Regulation S-X. The financial statements illustrated for iPayment are typical for a S-1 filing; they include comparative consolidated balance sheets (Exhibit 5-6) and statements of income (Exhibit 5-7), and statements of cash flows (Exhibit 5-8), all with appropriate footnotes and an auditor's report.

Exhibit 5-5: Business

Overview

We are a leading provider of credit and debit card-based payment processing services to small merchants. As of September 30, 2002, we provided our services to approximately 50,000 active small merchants located across the United States. The small merchants we serve typically generate less than $250,000 of charge volume per year and have an average transaction value of approximately $80. These merchants have traditionally been underserved by larger payment processors due to the difficulty in identifying, servicing and managing the risks associated with these merchants. As a result, these merchants have historically paid higher transaction fees than larger merchants.

Our payment processing services enable our merchants to process both traditional card-present, or "swipe," transactions, as well as card-not-present transactions. A traditional card-present transaction occurs whenever a cardholder physically presents a credit or debit card to a merchant at the point-of-sale. A card-not-present transaction occurs whenever the customer does not physically present a payment card at the point-of-sale and may occur over the Internet or by mail, fax or telephone.

We believe our experience and knowledge in providing payment processing services to small merchants give us the ability to effectively evaluate and manage the payment processing needs and risks that are unique to small businesses. In order to identify small merchants, we market and sell our services primarily through 500 independent sales organizations, or ISOs, representing approximately 2,000 sales people. ISOs allow us to access a large and experienced sales force with a local presence and access to small merchants over a broad geographic area without incurring the additional overhead costs associated with an internal sales force. We enable merchants to accept credit and debit cards as payment for their merchandise and services by providing processing, risk management, fraud detection, merchant assistance and support and chargeback services in connection with disputes with cardholders. In addition, we rely on third parties to provide card authorization, data capture, settlement and merchant accounting payment processing services, which allows us to maintain a scalable, efficient operating structure.

According to The Nilson Report's annual ranking of the top bank card acquirers in the United States in 2001, we were one of the fastest growing providers of card-based payment processing services. Our charge volume increased from approximately $459 million for the nine months ended September 30, 2001 to approximately $1,507 million for the nine months ended September 30, 2002. Similarly, our revenues increased from $23.6 million in the nine months ended September 30, 2001 to $67.3 million in the nine months ended September 30, 2002. This growth was primarily the result of our acquisitions of four card-based payment processors during 2002. For the three months ended September 30, 2002, revenues attributable to these acquisitions were $11.4 million, or 71.3% of our total growth in revenues over the prior period. We believe our ability to recruit and retain ISOs, combined with our experience in identifying, completing and integrating acquisitions, provides us with significant opportunities for future growth.

Industry Overview

The use of card-based forms of payment, such as credit and debit cards, by consumers in the United States has steadily increased over the past ten years. According to The Nilson Report, total expenditures of transactions by U.S. consumers using card-based systems grew from $0.5 trillion in 1991 to $1.8 trillion in 2001. The proliferation of credit and debit cards has made the acceptance of card based payment a necessity for businesses, both large and small, in order to remain competitive. Consumer expenditures using card-based payments methods are expected to grow to $4.2 trillion by 2011, or 48% of all U.S. payments, representing a compound annual growth rate of 9% from 2001 levels, according to The Nilson Report.

We believe that the card-based payment processing industry will continue to benefit from the following trends:

- **Favorable Demographics.** As consumers age, we expect that they will continue to use the payment technology to which they have grown accustomed. Consumers are beginning to use card-based and other electronic payment methods for purchases at an earlier age. According to Nellie Mae, the number of college students who have credit cards has grown from 67% in 1998 to 83% in 2001. As these consumers who have witnessed the wide adoption of card products, technology and the Internet comprise a greater percentage of the population and increasingly enter the work force, we expect that purchases using card-based payment methods will comprise an increasing percentage of total consumer spending.
- **Increased Card Acceptance by Small Businesses.** Small businesses are a vital component of the U.S. economy and are expected to contribute to the increased use of card-based payments methods. The U.S. Census Bureau estimates that approximately 20 million businesses with on average less than $1.0 million in annual sales in the United States, generate an aggregate of $1.7 trillion in annual sales. The lower costs associated with card-based payment methods are making these services more affordable to a larger segment of the small business market. In addition, we believe these businesses are experiencing increased pressure to accept card-based payment methods in order to remain competitive and to meet consumer expectations. As a result, many of these small businesses are seeking, and we expect many new small businesses to seek, to provide customers with the ability to pay for merchandise and services using credit or debit cards, including those in industries that have historically accepted cash and checks as the only forms of payment for their merchandise and services.
- **Growth in Card-Not-Present Transactions.** Market researchers expect dramatic growth in card-not-present transactions due to the rapid growth of the Internet. According to Jupiter Media Corporation, 94% of the dollar value of all merchandise and services ordered online by consumers in 2003 will be purchased using card-based systems. In total, IDC, an independent market intelligence firm, expects U.S. consumer electronic commerce to grow from $66.6 billion in 2001 to $322.8 billion in 2006, representing a compound annual growth rate of 37.1%. In addition, IDC estimates that approximately two-thirds of all small businesses have online capabilities. The prevalence of the Internet makes having an online presence a basic consideration for those forming a new business today.

Source: <http://www.sec.gov/Archives/edgar/data/1140184/000095012302011600/y65042sv1.htm>

Exhibit 5-6: Consolidated Balance Sheets

iPAYMENT, INC.

	December 31, 2000	December 31, 2001	September 30, 2002
	(dollars in thousands, except share amounts)		
ASSETS			
Current assets:			
Cash and cash equivalents	$ 568	$ 290	$ 1,387
Accounts receivable, net of allowance for doubtful accounts of $130, $225, and $52 as of December 31, 2000, December 31, 2001 and September 30, 2002, respectively	753	1,920	6,762
Prepaid expenses and other current assets	15	453	2,776
Total current assets	1,336	2,663	10,925
Restricted cash	282	687	4,993
Property and equipment, net	604	973	1,572
Intangible assets, net	4,284	19,710	30,299
Goodwill, net	6,795	11,041	56,450
Other assets	68	1,007	6,013
Total assets	$ 13,369	$ 36,081	$ 110,252

LIABILITIES, MANDATORILY REDEEMABLE CONVERTIBLE PREFERRED STOCK AND STOCKHOLDERS' EQUITY (DEFICIT)

Current liabilities:			
Reserve for losses on merchant accounts	202	$ 3,165	$ 6,790
Accounts payable and accrued liabilities	6,174	4,041	16,996
Current portion of long-term debt	9,053	4,274	9,674
Total current liabilities	15,429	11,480	33,460
Long-term liabilities:			
Long-term debt, net of current portion and discount	2,876	28,526	59,797
Other long-term liabilities	2,331	1,912	2,091
Total long-term liabilities	5,207	30,438	61,888
Total liabilities	20,636	41,918	95,348

Commitments and contingencies (Note 13) Mandatorily redeemable convertible preferred stock, no par value; 10,000,000 shares authorized, zero, 2,577,200 and 2,577,200 shares issued and outstanding at December 31, 2000, December 31, 2001 and September 30, 2002, respectively	—	5,154	6,250
Stockholders' Equity (Deficit):			
Common stock, no par value; 40,000,000 shares authorized, 2,777,130, 9,683,190, and 14,558,190 shares issued and outstanding at December 31, 2000, December 31, 2001, and September 30, 2002, respectively	1,152	3,192	24,067
Deferred compensation	—	—	(40)
Accumulated deficit	(8,419)	(14,183)	(15,373)
Total stockholders' equity (deficit)	(7,267)	(10,991)	8,654
Total liabilities and stockholders' equity (deficit)	13,369 $	36,081 $	110,252

Source: <http://www.sec.gov/Archives/edgar/data/1140184/000095012302011600/y65042sv1.htm>

Exhibit 5-7: Consolidated Statements of Operations

iPAYMENT, INC.

	Predecessor Company		Successor Company		
	Period from January 1, 2000 through July 19, 2000	July 20, 2000 Through December 31, 2000	Year Ended December 31, 2001	Nine Months Ended September 30, 2001	Nine Months Ended September 30, 2002
				(unaudited)	
	(dollars in thousands, except per share data)				
Revenues	$12,870	$7,835	$38,889	$23,634	$67,268
Operating expenses:					
Cost of services	12,360	6,668	33,633	18,447	54,734
Selling, general and administrative	2,040	4,546	3,782	2,373	4,488
Depreciation and amortization	477	2,351	4,299	3,011	3,759
Restructuring costs	—	1,585	(131)	—	—
Total operating expenses	14,877	15,150	41,583	23,831	62,981
Income (loss) from operations	(2,007)	(7,315)	(2,694)	(197)	4,287

Other income (expense):					
Interest expense	(109)	(706)	(2,928)	(1,564)	(3,914)
Other	(15)	(397)	625	631	(1)
Total other expense	(124)	(1,103)	(2,303)	(933)	(3,915)
Income (loss) before income taxes	(2,131)	(8,418)	(4,997)	(1,130)	372
Income tax provision (benefit)	1	1	(107)	3	466
Net loss	(2,132)	(8,419)	(4,890)	(1,133)	(94)
Accretion of mandatorily redeemable convertible preferred stock	—	—	(874)	(550)	(1,096)
Net loss available to common stockholders$	(2,132)	$(8,419)	$(5,764)	$(1,683)	$(1,190)
Basic and diluted loss per common share:					
Loss per share	$(43.60)	$(5.84)	$(0.65)	$(0.20)	$(0.12)
Weighted average shares outstanding	48,899	1,440,457	8,862,727	8,589,240	10,286,888

Source: http://www.sec.gov/Archives/edgar/data/1140184/000095012302011600/y65042sv1.htm

Exhibit 5-8

iPAYMENT, INC.

CONSOLIDATED STATEMENTS OF CASH FLOWS

	Predecessor Company	Successor Company			
	Period from January 1, 2000 through July 19, 2000	Period from July 20, 2000 through December 31, 2000	Year Ended December 31, 2001	Nine Months Ended September 30, 2001	Nine Months Ended September 30, 2002
				(unaudited)	
		(dollars in thousands)			
Cash flows from operating activities:					
Net loss	$ (2,132)	$ (8,419)	$ (4,890)	$ (1,133)	$ (94)
Adjustments to reconcile net loss to net cash used in operating activities:					
Depreciation and amortization	477	2,351	4,299	3,011	3,759
Impairment of contract costs	—	2,070	—	—	—
Impairment of property and equipment	—	842	—	—	—
Impairment of intangible assets	—	375	—	—	74
Loss on sale of equipment	20	91	20	—	—
Accrual for merchant losses	—	26	2,963	249	3,179

Provision for allowance for doubtful accounts	—	82	95	—	—
Income taxes	—	—	(112)	(3)	466
Amortization of debt warrants discount	—	—	338	—	728
Issuance of common stock to employees for services rendered	3	4	22	22	20
Amortization of debt issuance costs	—	—	122	—	124
ECP debt amortization	(498)	—	—	—	—
Changes in assets and liabilities:					
Accounts receivable	534	(480)	(1,262)	(983)	(2,519)
Prepaid expenses and other current assets	(32)	66	(438)	(76)	(444)
Other assets	58	(18)	(1,061)	(2,376)	(3,141)
Accounts payable and accrued liabilities	890	1,994	(1,956)	(1,606)	(2,000)
Other liabilities	(311)	—	(307)	(104)	179
Net cash (used in) provided by operating activities	(991)	(1,016)	(2,167)	(2,999)	331
Cash flows from investing activities:					
Change in restricted cash	(198)	(5)	(405)	(140)	(2,751)
Expenditures for property and equipment	(397)	(8)	(386)	(76)	(188)
Expenditures for acquisitions of	—	(400)	(9,148)	(9,148)	(994)

intangible assets					
Acquisitions of businesses, net of cash received	—	—	(11,194)	(11,194)	(4,276)
Net cash used in investing activities	(595)	(413)	(21,133)	(20,558)	(8,209)
Cash flows from financing activities:					
Principal payments under capital lease obligations	(70)	(57)	(237)	(175)	(154)
Distribution to shareholder	(496)	—	—	—	—
Proceeds from issuances of long-term debt	2,222	1,400	25,599	25,599	14,203
Repayments of long-term debt	(163)	(462)	(5,127)	(5,028)	(5,074)
Proceeds from issuance of preferred stock	—	—	2,750	2,750	—
Proceeds from issuance of common stock	173	1,023	37	37	—
Net cash provided by financing activities	1,666	1,904	23,022	23,183	8,975
Net increase (decrease) in cash and cash equivalents	80	475	(278)	(374)	1,097
Cash and cash equivalents, beginning of period	13	93	568	568	290
Cash and cash equivalents, end of period	$ 93	$ 568	$ 290	$ 194	$ 1,387

iPAYMENT, INC.

CONSOLIDATED STATEMENTS OF CASH FLOWS — (Continued)

	Predecessor Company	Successor Company			
	Period from January 1, 2000 through July 19, 2000	Period from July 20, 2000 through December 31, 2000	Year Ended December 31, 2001	Nine Months Ended September 30, 2001	Nine Months Ended September 30, 2002
				(unaudited)	
	(dollars in thousands)				
Supplemental disclosure of cash flow information:					
Cash paid during the period for income taxes	$ 3	$ 6	$ 68	$ 68	$ 7
Cash paid during the period for interest	$ 97	$ 193	$ 2,368	$ 1,588	$ 2,975
Supplemental disclosure of noncash investing and financing activities:					
Conversion of debt to equity	$ —	$ —	$ 1,950	$ 1,950	$ —
Additions of equipment leases	$ 10	$ 20	$ —	$ —	$ —
Exchange of common stock to mandatorily redeemable preferred stock	$ —	$ —	$ 1,530	$ 1,530	$ —

Accretion of mandatorily redeemable convertible preferred stock	$ 1,096	$ 550	$ 874	$ —
Acquisition of businesses funded with:				
Debt	$ 22,099	$ 2,954	$ 2,954	$ —
Common stock	$ 17,355	$ 678	$ 678	$ —
Non-cash increase in assets and liabilities from acquisitions:				
Restricted cash	$ 1,555	$ —	$ —	$ —
Accounts receivable	$ 2,323	$ —	$ —	$ —
Other assets	$ 1,972	$ —	$ —	$ —
Plant and equipment	$ 768	$ 275	$ 275	$ —
Intangible assets	$ 13,290	$ 9,957	$ 9,957	$ —
Goodwill	$ 45,409	$ 4,594	$ 4,594	$ —
Accounts payable, accrued liabilities and merchant loss reserve	$ 11,159	$ —	$ —	$ —
Short and long term debt	$ 10,428	$ —	$ —	$ —
Non-cash effect of Reorganization:				
Increase in intangible assets	$ —	$ —	$ —	$ 3,550
Increase in long term and short-term debt	$ —	$ —	$ —	$ 3,083

The other forms used for registration under the 1933 Act require additional specialized information as circumstances of the registrant change, but the basic disclosure of a company's business and financial position is common to all forms.

REGISTRATION AND REPORTING UNDER THE 1934 ACT

Registration under the 1934 Act is a twofold process. Before securities can be traded in the secondary markets, a registration statement must be on file with both the SEC and the exchange on which the securities are to be traded. This requirement holds true even if a registration was made under the 1933 Act. Besides the dual registration, annual and other periodic reports are necessary. These provide a current record of all companies whose securities are traded. When securities are traded on over-the-counter markets, a registration with the SEC also is required—except for small companies—and the periodic reporting requirements must be met.

Registration requirements under the Securities Exchange Act of 1934 are almost identical to those of the Securities Act of 1933, so a review is not provided here. However, when a company registers its securities with an exchange, the information required may be somewhat different.

Chapter 4 lists the forms used for registration with the SEC, and these forms are substantially duplicated for registering with the exchanges. Of particular interest are (1) a review of the reporting documents submitted annually and quarterly to the SEC, and (2) a comparison of these reports with the annual and quarterly reports to stockholders. Information disclosed in reports to shareholders is expected to closely resemble the information in reports filed with the SEC.

Annual Reports

The most common SEC annual report form is Form 10-K. This report must be filed within 90 days of the end of a company's fiscal year. Form 10-K is used to update the information a company gives with the registration statement; hence, the format is similar to that of an S-1. However, with the implementation of the SEC's integrated disclosure system, Form 10-K has been revised significantly. Exhibit 5-9 compares the required disclosure items for Form 10-K to the required items for Form S-1:

Exhibit 5-9: Comparison of Form 10-K and Form S-1

Items Required in Part I and Part II	Items Required in Form 10-K
Part I	
1. Forepart of the Registration Statement and Outside Front Cover Page of Prospectus	1. General instructions
	2. Cover page
2. Inside Front and Outside Back Cover Pages of Prospectus	3. Disclosures relating to a company's business, properties, legal proceedings, and matters requiring submission for a vote of security holders (Part I)
3. Summary Information, Risk Factors, and Ratio of Earnings to Fixed Charges	
4. Use of Proceeds	4. Information required by proxy rules to be included in the annual report to shareholders, such as market price data, selected financial data, three years of audited financial statements, management's discussion and analysis of the company's financial condition and results of operations, supplementary financial data, and information concerning disagreements on accounting and financial disclosures (Part II)
5. Determination of Offering Price	
6. Dilution	
7. Selling Security Holders	
8. Plan of Distribution	
9. Description of Securities to Be Registered	
10. Interest of Named Experts and Counsel	
11. Information with Respect to the Registrant (including such items as description of business, property, legal proceedings, financial statements, supplements, financial information, management's discussion and analysis, changes in accountants and executive compensation.)	5. Traditional proxy disclosure information relating to directors and executive officers, and management's remuneration (Part III)
12. Disclosure of Commission Position on Indemnification for Securities Act Liabilities	

| Part II | 6. | Financial statements not |

Part II

13. Other Expenses of Issuance of Distribution

14. Indemnification of Directors and Officers

15. Recent Sales of Unregistered Securities

16. Exhibits and Financial Statement Schedules

17. Undertakings

6. Financial statements not required in the annual reports to shareholders and additional financial schedules and exhibits (Part IV)

7. Signatures

8. Supplemental information

Sources: <http://www.sec.gov/about/forms/forms-1.pdf> and <http://www.sec.gov/about/forms/form10-k.pdf>

Much of the information in the Form 10-K may be incorporated by reference. For example, the financial statements from the annual report to shareholders frequently are incorporated by reference in Form 10-K. This is again in keeping with the SEC's attempt to reduce duplicate disclosures and to integrate and simplify its reporting requirements. The content of the four main parts of Form 10-K is given in Exhibit 5-10.

Exhibit 5-10: Disclosure Items for Form 10-K

Part I

Item 1. Business

Item 2. Properties

Item 3. Legal Proceedings

Item 4. Submission of Matters to a Vote of Security Holders

Part II

Item 5. Market for the Registrant's Common Equity and Related Stockholder Matters

Item 6. Selected Financial Data

Item 7. Management's Discussion and Analysis of Financial Condition and Results of Operations Risk

Item 7A. Quantitative and Qualitative Disclosures About Market

Item 8. Financial Statements and Supplementary Data
Item 9. Changes in and Disagreements with Accountants on Accounting and Financial Disclosure
Item 9A. Disclosure Controls and Procedures

Part III
  Item 10. Directors and Executive Officers of the Registrant
  Item 11. Executive Compensation
  Item 12. Security Ownership of Certain Beneficial Owners and Management and Related Stockholder Matters
  Item 13. Certain Relationships and Related Transactions
  Item 14. Controls and Procedures

Part IV
  Item 15. Exhibits, Financial Statement Schedules and Reports on Form 8-K

Source: http://www.sec.gov/about/forms/form10-k.pdf

Item 1 (Business) covers the same broad overview of company operations given in a Form S-1 and comprises the major part of the narrative in the Form 10-K. The annual report to stockholders generally does not present such a lengthy discussion, but it is designed to summarize for the investor the business of the firm.

An important section of the Form 10-K is management's discussion and analysis of the financial condition and results of operations as required by item 7. However, as was mentioned earlier, this information may be incorporated by reference to other reports and is not required to be duplicated. For example, Cisco Systems, Inc. made the statements shown in Exhibit 5-11 relative to items 6, 7, and 8. Because the SEC allows incorporation by reference, the Form 10-Ks of companies are becoming smaller and the information in annual reports to shareholders is expanding.

Exhibit 5-11

ITEM 6.

Selected Financial Data

The information required by this item is incorporated by reference to page 17 of our 2003 Annual Report to Shareholders.

ITEM 7.

Management's Discussion and Analysis of Financial Condition and Results of Operations

The information required by this item is incorporated by reference to pages 18 to 32 of our 2003 Annual Report to Shareholders.

ITEM 7A.

Quantitative and Qualitative Disclosures About Market Risk

The information required by this item is incorporated by reference to pages 33 to 34 of our 2003 Annual Report to Shareholders.

ITEM 8.

Financial Statements and Supplementary Data

The information required by this item is incorporated by reference to pages 35 to 63 of our 2003 Annual Report to Shareholders.

Source: <http://www.sec.gov/Archives/edgar/data/858877/000119312503047374/d10k.htm#tx79151_18>

Other critical parts of the Form 10-K include the certifications of the chief executive and chief financial officers which are submitted as exhibits to the 10-K. Exhibit 5-12 demonstrates one of the several certifications that are currently required: the certification of the chief executive officer under Section 302 of the Sarbanes-Oxley Act. The exhibit shows that this certification is quite extensive, in that the CEO must certify the accuracy of the financial statements, the adequacy of the disclosure controls and procedures, and certain internal controls matters. These certifications serve to increase the emphasis on the key role of upper management in effective corporate governance, especially given that these certifications are just a few of many that executives of public companies either must now make, or will shortly need to make as the full implementation of the Sarbanes-Oxley Act unfolds.

Exhibit 5-12

CERTIFICATION OF PRINCIPAL EXECUTIVE OFFICER PURSUANT TO EXCHANGE ACT RULE 13a-14(a)/15d-14(a) AS ADOPTED PURSUANT TO SECTION 302 OF THE SARBANES-OXLEY ACT OF 2002

I, John T. Chambers, President and Chief Executive Officer of Cisco Systems, Inc., certify that:

1. I have reviewed this annual report on Form 10-K of Cisco Systems, Inc.;

2. Based on my knowledge, this report does not contain any untrue statement of a material fact or omit to state a material fact necessary to make the statements made, in light of the circumstances under which such statements were made, not misleading with respect to the period covered by this report;

3. Based on my knowledge, the financial statements, and other financial information included in this report, fairly present in all material respects the financial condition, results of operations and cash flows of the registrant as of, and for, the periods presented in this report;

4. The registrant's other certifying officer(s) and I are responsible for establishing and maintaining disclosure controls and procedures (as defined in Exchange Act Rules 13a-15(e) and 15d-15(e)) for the registrant and have:

   (a) Designed such disclosure controls and procedures, or caused such disclosure controls and procedures to be designed under our supervision, to ensure that material information relating to the registrant, including its consolidated subsidiaries, is made known to us by others within those entities, particularly during the period in which this report is being prepared;

   (b) Evaluated the effectiveness of the registrant's disclosure controls and procedures and presented in this report our conclusions about the effectiveness of the disclosure controls and procedures, as of the end of the period covered by this report based on such evaluation; and

   (c) Disclosed in this report any change in the registrant's internal control over financial reporting that occurred during the registrant's most recent fiscal quarter (the registrant's fourth fiscal quarter in the case of an annual report) that has materially affected, or is reasonably likely to materially affect, the registrant's internal control over financial reporting; and

5. The registrant's other certifying officer(s) and I have disclosed, based on our most recent evaluation of internal control over financial reporting, to the registrant's auditors and the audit committee of the registrant's board of directors (or persons performing the equivalent functions):

   (a) All significant deficiencies and material weaknesses in the design or operation of internal control over financial reporting which are reasonably likely to adversely affect the registrant's ability to record, process, summarize and report financial information; and

   (b) Any fraud, whether or not material, that involves management or other employees who have a significant role in the registrant's internal control over financial reporting.

Date: September 9, 2003

/s/   JOHN T. CHAMBERS

John T. Chambers
President and Chief Executive Officer
(Principal Executive Officer)

Source: <http://www.sec.gov/Archives/edgar/data/858877/000119312503047374/dex311.htm>

Quarterly Reports

To keep both investors and experts apprised of interim changes in a company's operations and financial position, quarterly reports are prepared for stockholders and the SEC. From time to time, the SEC changes this form in order to make the Form 10-Q more useful to analysts and investors. The financial data currently required parallel closely the disclosures required in annual reports to the SEC, except that the Form 10-Q contains only quarterly information. Consistent with its philosophy of integration, published quarterly stockholder reports may be incorporated by reference in satisfaction of Form 10-Q requirements, provided the SEC requirements are met.

All quarterly data should be prepared in accordance with generally accepted accounting principles as specified by the FASB and other authoritative accounting bodies. APB Opinion No. 28, SFAS No. 3, and rule 10-01 of Regulation S-X provide reporting guidelines on preparing interim statements for Form 10-Q submission. Form 10-Q must be filed within 45 days after the end of each of the registrant's first three quarters; a Form 10-Q is not required for the fourth quarter since the full-year annual report will be provided shortly. The information to be included in Part I and Part II of Form 10-Q is listed in Exhibit 5-13.

Exhibit 5-13: Items Required for Parts I and II of Form 10-Q

Part I—Financial Information	Part II—Other Information
1. Financial Statements	1. Legal Proceedings
2. Management's Discussion and Analysis of Financial Condition and Results of Operations	2. Changes in Securities and Use of Proceeds
3. Quantitative and Qualitative Disclosures About Market Risk	3. Defaults upon Senior Securities
4. Controls and Procedures	4. Submission of Matters to a Vote of Security Holders
	5. Other Information
	6. Exhibits and Reports on Form 8-K

Source: <http://www.sec.gov/about/forms/form10-q.pdf>

An example of a Form 10-Q is provided in Exhibit 5-14. Please note that the financial statements are unaudited and that the accountant's report clearly states that a review, not an audit, has been made.

Exhibit 5-14: An Example of Form 10-Q

UNITED STATES
SECURITIES AND EXCHANGE COMMISSION

Washington, D.C. 20549

FORM 10-Q

QUARTERLY REPORTS UNDER SECTION 13 OR 15(d) OF
THE SECURITIES AND EXCHANGE ACT OF 1934

For the Quarter Ended August 31, 2002
Commission file number - 1-10635

NIKE, Inc.

(Exact name of registrant as specified in its charter)

OREGON   93-0584541

(State or other jurisdiction of   (I.R.S. Employer
incorporation or organization)   Identification No.)

One Bowerman Drive, Beaverton, Oregon   97005-6453

(Address of principal executive offices) (Zip Code)

Registrant's telephone number, including area code (503) 671-6453

Indicate by check mark whether the registrant (1) has filed all reports
required to be filed by Section 13 or 15 (d) of the Securities Exchange Act of
1934 during the preceding 12 months (or for such shorter period that the
registrant was required to file such reports), and (2) has been subject to such
filing requirements for the past 90 days

Yes X No   .

Common Stock shares outstanding as of August 31, 2002 were:

Class A	98,095,361
Class B	167,184,833
	265,280,194

```
PART 1 - FINANCIAL INFORMATION
Item 1.  FINANCIAL STATEMENTS
                              NIKE, Inc.
                  CONDENSED CONSOLIDATED BALANCE SHEET
August 31,                              May 31,
  2002     2002
          (in millions)
ASSETS
Current assets:
  Cash and equivalents                      $   430.0    $     575.5
  Accounts receivable                         2,028.0        1,807.1
  Inventories (Note 5)                        1,424.8        1,373.8
  Deferred income taxes                         171.6          140.8
  Prepaid expenses and other current assets     249.9          260.5

  Total current assets                         4,304.3        4,157.7
Property, plant and equipment                  2,814.9        2,741.7
  Less accumulated depreciation                1,189.1        1,127.2

                                               1,625.8        1,614.5
Identifiable intangible assets and goodwill (Note 2)  184.8     438.7
Deferred income taxes and other assets          241.0          232.1

                                             $6,355.9       $6,443.0
                                             ========       ========
LIABILITIES AND SHAREHOLDERS' EQUITY
Current liabilities:
  Current portion of long-term debt         $    5.6     $     55.3
  Notes payable                                 217.4          425.2
  Accounts payable                              486.6          504.4
  Accrued liabilities                           917.5          768.3
  Income taxes payable                          159.5           83.0

  Total current liabilities                   1,786.6        1,836.2
Long-term debt                                  736.3          625.9
Deferred income taxes and other liabilities     160.2          141.6
Commitments and contingencies (Note 7)           --             --
Redeemable preferred stock                        0.3            0.3
Shareholders' equity:
  Common stock at stated value:
  Class A convertible-98.1 and
  98.1 shares outstanding                         0.2            0.2
  Class B-167.2 and 168.0 shares
    outstanding                                   2.6            2.6
  Capital in excess of stated value             543.8          538.7
  Unearned stock compensation                    (3.7)          (5.1)
  Accumulated other comprehensive income       (241.3)        (192.4)
  Retained earnings                           3,370.9        3,495.0

  Total shareholders' equity                  3,672.5        3,839.0

                                             $6,355.9       $ 6,443.0
                                             ========       ========
```

NIKE, Inc.

NOTES TO CONDENSED CONSOLIDATED FINANCIAL STATEMENTS

NOTE 1 - Summary of Significant Accounting Policies:

Basis of presentation:

   The accompanying unaudited condensed consolidated financial statements reflect all adjustments (consisting of normal recurring accruals) which are, in the opinion of management, necessary for a fair presentation of the results of operations for the interim period. The interim financial information and notes thereto should be read in conjunction with the Company's latest Annual Report on Form 10-K. The results of operations for the three (3) months ended August 31, 2002 are not necessarily indicative of results to be expected for the entire year.

   Certain prior year amounts have been reclassified to conform to fiscal year 2003 presentation. These changes had no impact on previously reported results of operations or shareholders' equity.

NOTE 2 - Identifiable Intangible Assets and Goodwill:

Adoption of FAS 142

   The Company adopted Statement of Financial Accounting Standards No. 142, Goodwill and Other Intangible Assets," (FAS 142) effective June 1, 2002. In accordance with FAS 142, goodwill and intangible assets with indefinite lives will no longer be amortized but instead will be measured for impairment at least annually, or when events indicate that an impairment exists. Intangible assets that are determined to have definite lives will continue to be amortized over their useful lives.

   As required by FAS 142, the Company performed impairment tests on goodwill and other intangible assets with indefinite lives, which consisted only of certain trademarks, as of June 1, 2002. As a result of the impairment tests, the Company recorded a $266.1 million cumulative effect of accounting change. Under FAS 142, goodwill impairment exists if the net book value of a reporting unit exceeds its estimated fair value. The Company estimated the fair value of its reporting units by using a combination of discounted cash flow analyses and comparisons with the market values of similar publicly-traded companies.

Source: <http://www.sec.gov/Archives/edgar/data/320187/000032018702000021/t1q0310q.txt>

Form 8-K

Quarterly reports are submitted following the first three quarters of a company's reporting year. The annual report then consolidates the year's operations. Between these periodic filings, significant changes may take place in either a firm's policies or its financial position. To ensure adequate disclosure of any such material event, Form 8-K, the so-called current report, generally must be submitted to the SEC within 4 business days after the occurrence of a significant event. Form 8-K generally does not require certified financial data. Financial statements accompany Form 8-K only when the form is submitted pursuant to an acquisition, and then only when the acquired company represents more than 20 percent of the total assets or revenues of the registering company. The information provided in Form 8-K is mostly narrative and is intended to keep prospective shareholders (and the SEC) informed of significant developments on a timely basis.

As Chapter 3 mentioned, the SEC Release No. 34-8400 issued in March 2004 substantially increased the scope and timeliness of 8-K filings. This release also reorganized the numbering of Form 8-K. The SEC Release was in response to section 409 of the Sarbanes-Oxley Act of 2002 which requires "real time" disclosure of material events. Prior to this release, Form 8-K was filed either 15 days or 5 days after a triggering event, depending on the nature of the event. Exhibit 5-15 summarizes the changes in the organization and in the nature of triggering events that require a Form 8-K filing under these new final rules.

Exhibit 5-15: Form 8-K'S Reorganization

The new rule reorganizes Form 8-K, using the following section headings and numbering:

Section 1 – Registrant's Business and Operations
    Item 1.01 Entry into a Material Definitive Agreement*
    Item 1.02 Termination of a Material Definitive Agreement*
    Item 1.03 Bankruptcy or Receivership
Section 2 – Financial Information
    Item 2.01 Completion of Acquisition or Disposition of Assets
    Item 2.02 Results of Operations and Financial Condition
    Item 2.03 Creation of a Direct Financial Obligation or an Obligation under an Off-Balance Sheet Arrangement of a Registrant*
    Item 2.04 Triggering Events That Accelerate or Increase a Direct Financial Obligation or an Obligation under an Off-Balance Sheet Arrangement*
    Item 2.05 Costs Associated with Exit or Disposal Activities*
    Item 2.06 Material Impairments*
Section 3 – Securities and Trading Markets
    Item 3.01 Notice of Delisting or Failure to Satisfy a Continued Listing Rule or Standard; Transfer of Listing*
    Item 3.02 Unregistered Sales of Equity Securities**

Item 3.03 Material Modifications to Rights of Security Holders**
Section 4 – Matters Related to Accountants and Financial Statements
Item 4.01 Changes in Registrant's Certifying Accountant
Item 4.02 Non-Reliance on Previously Issued Financial Statements or a
Related Audit Report or Completed Interim Review*
Section 5 – Corporate Governance and Management
Item 5.01 Changes in Control of Registrant
Item 5.02 Departure of Directors or Principal Officers; Election of
Directors, Appointment of Principal Officers***
Item 5.03 Amendments to Articles of Incorporation or Bylaws; Change
in Fiscal Year***
Item 5.04 Temporary Suspension of Trading Under Registrant's
Employee Benefit Plans
Item 5.05 Amendments to the Registrant's Code of Ethics, or Waiver of
a Provision of the Code of Ethics

* New triggering events.
**Reported events new to the Form 8-K, transferred from other filings.
***Scope of a triggering event expanded.

Adapted from "More Form 8-K Disclosures, Less Filing Time," *KPMG's Defining Issues,*
March 2004, No. 04-6.

As with all other SEC forms, the 8-K has no specific format but is a narrative report of sufficient flexibility to permit management to describe any changes that may affect the firm. Financial statements accompany Form 8-K only when the form is submitted pursuant to an acquisition, and then only when the acquired company represents more than 20 percent of the total assets or revenues of the registering company. Exhibit 5-16 presents an example of Form 8-K before the changes were instituted under Release No. 34-8400; the reader should note the brief nature of this example 8-K, and the use of reference by incorporation. Examples of Form 8-K's filed under the new rule can be accessed through the SEC's EDGAR database (see appendix at the end of Chapter 4 for information regarding accessing forms on EDGAR).

Exhibit 5-16: An Example of Form 8-K

SECURITIES AND EXCHANGE COMMISSION
Washington, D.C. 20549

FORM 8-K

CURRENT REPORT
Pursuant to Section 13 or 15(d) of the
Securities Exchange Act of 1934

Date of Report (Date of earliest event reported):
October 25, 2002

NIKE, INC.

(Exact Name of Registrant as Specified in Charter)

Oregon	1-10635	93-0584541
(State of Incorporation)	(Commission File Number)	(I.R.S.Employer Identification No.)

One Bowerman Drive
Beaverton, Oregon 97005-6453

(Address of Principal Executive Offices)

(503) 671-6453

(Registrant's telephone number, including area code)

Item 5.   OTHER EVENTS

Today NIKE, Inc. issued the following press release:

NIKE REACHES AGREEMENT TO SETTLE SECURITIES CLASS
ACTION LAWSUITS

Beaverton, OR (October 25, 2002) - Nike, Inc. (NYSE,
NKE) announced today that it has reached an agreement
to settle the securities class action lawsuits that
have been consolidated under the caption In re _____
Nike, Inc. Securities Litigation, Master File No. CV-
01-332-KI in the _____ United

States District Court for the District of Oregon.
The agreement is reflected in a memorandum of
understanding, and must be incorporated into more
complete settlement documentation and approved by the
court. Nike will pay $8.9 million in cash, which will
be funded by the Company's directors and officers
liability insurance. In the agreement, Nike and the
officers and directors named in the lawsuits do not
admit, and continue to deny, any and all allegations
of wrongdoing, and that they will receive a full
release of all claims asserted in the litigation.

NIKE, Inc., based in Beaverton, Oregon, is the
world's leading designer and marketer of authentic
athletic footwear, apparel, equipment and accessories
for a wide variety of sports and fitness activities.
Wholly owned NIKE subsidiaries include Bauer NIKE
Hockey Inc., the world's leading manufacturer of
hockey equipment; Cole Haan (registered), which
markets a line of high-quality men's and women's
dress and casual shoes; and Hurley International LLC,
which markets action sports and teen lifestyle
apparel.

NIKE's earnings releases and other financial
information are available on the Internet at
NikeBiz.com.

Precautionary Language Regarding Forward-
Looking Statements

This press release contains statements,
including those describing the terms and consummation
of the settlement agreement described above, that
constitute forward-looking statements within the
meaning of Section 21(E) of the Securities Exchange
Act of 1934. The statements are subject to certain
risks and uncertainties, including but not limited to
the risk that the settlement may not be approved by
the court, or might not be consummated for other
reasons, and the risk that a significant number of
investors covered by the settlement may "opt out" of
the agreement and pursue separate claims against the
Company and/or the individual defendants. Nike
undertakes no duty to update any of the statements
set forth in this release.

SIGNATURES

Pursuant to the requirements of the Securities
Exchange Act of 1934, the registrant has duly caused
this report to be signed on its behalf by the
undersigned hereunto duly authorized.

NIKE, Inc.
(Registrant)

Date: October 25, 2002
/s/ Donald W. Blair
_____
By: Donald W. Blair
Chief Financial Officer

Source: http://www.sec.gov/Archives/edgar/data/320187/ 000032018702000025/l02_10-258k.txt

SUMMARY

In Chapter 4 we provided an overview of the registration process and introduced various registration forms. In Chapter 5, we provide content guidelines and illustrations for forms most commonly used for SEC registration and reporting.

Over the past several years, disclosure to stockholders has been enhanced significantly. Much of the improvement has come as a result of SEC prompting, but management teams have also responded on their own initiative to provide stockholders with more adequate information. Although the detailed reporting is tedious, the result is that even relatively sophisticated investors are supplied with the necessary information to make their investing decisions.

DISCUSSION QUESTIONS

1. How many different annual reports do managements prepare? To whom do these reports go?

2. What are some of the more important disclosure requirements for annual reports?

3.   What are the most common forms prepared for the SEC? What information do they contain?

4.   What is the nature of Form 8-K?

5.   In what ways is financial reporting to the SEC different from financial reporting to shareholders?

6.   What are the certifications required of the CEO under rules 302 and 404 of the Sarbanes-Oxley Act of 2002, and what is the intended purpose of requiring the CEO to make these certifications?

6

Impact of the SEC on Financial Reporting, Auditing, and Corporate Governance

Two interesting and important topics concerning the influence of the SEC are (1) the role the SEC plays in the development of financial reporting and auditing standards and (2) the impact the SEC has had and continues to have on the accounting profession and corporate governance in general. The variety of responsibilities discussed in earlier chapters, pursuant to the SEC's broad statutory powers, clearly makes the SEC an important player in the business community in its efforts to enhance corporate governance.

In this chapter, the SEC's authority and influence with respect to corporate governance, financial reporting, and auditing is examined. A discussion of accounting practices arising as a result of this legal authority is also presented. Finally, the interaction of the SEC with the accounting profession in developing accounting and auditing standards is discussed.

SEC AUTHORITY RELATIVE TO FINANCIAL REPORTING PRACTICE

As noted in Chapter 3, the SEC has the statutory authority to regulate and to prescribe the form, content, and compilation process of financial statements and other reports filed with the commission and disseminated to shareholders and the investing public. The SEC's responsibilities and authority with respect to financial accounting, reporting, and auditing was granted by Congress. This authority has led to a close and continued interaction between the SEC and the accounting profession. This chapter illustrates how the SEC has played a significant role in the development of financial accounting and reporting principles and practices as well as auditing standards and procedures. Appreciation of the interaction between the SEC and the professions involved in the financial reporting process is sometimes lacking among business professionals and accounting students.

Congressional Authority

Congress recognized that the SEC would need some control of accounting principles and procedures in order to fulfill its goal of full and fair disclosure. The regulatory authority given to the SEC was influenced considerably by the wide variation in accepted accounting principles and procedures that existed in the late 1920s. Some observers felt that this variation may have contributed to the stock market crash and to the decline of the economy in general. In any event, Congress wanted to provide adequate disclosure of information for investors and gave the SEC authority to prescribe the accounting principles and procedures to be used in the financial statements it receives.

Congressional Acts. The first Congressional grant of accounting authority was to the Federal Trade Commission (FTC) in the Securities Act of 1933. Section 19(a) of the Act delineates this responsibility:

> . . . [T]he Commission shall have authority . . . to prescribe the form or forms in which required information shall be set forth, the items or details to be shown in the balance sheet and earning statement, and the methods to be followed in the preparation of accounts, in the appraisal or valuation of assets and liabilities, in the determination of depreciation and depletion, in the

differentiation of recurring and nonrecurring income, in the differentiation of investment and operating income, and in the preparation, where the Commission deems it necessary or desirable, of consolidated balance sheets or income accounts . . . .

Thus, the 1933 Act gave the FTC broad powers to prescribe any forms, rules, procedures, and regulations it deemed necessary to fulfill its obligations under the law. Included is the authority to have the last word on any accounting matter related to companies filing under the Act.

With the 1934 Act and the formation of the SEC, the SEC inherited this authority from the FTC and received additional authority to regulate companies filing periodic reports. Section 13(b) of the 1934 Act states:

The Commission [SEC] may prescribe, in regard to reports made pursuant to this title [chapter], the form or forms in which the required information shall be set forth, the items or details to be shown in the balance sheet and the earning statement, and the methods to be followed in the preparation of reports, in the appraisal or valuation of assets and liabilities . . . .

The section continues in a manner similar to that of the 1933 Act. Thus, the regulatory powers given to the SEC relative to accounting practice under the 1934 Act are comparable to those given to the FTC under the 1933 Act.

It is important to recognize that the SEC's authority extends only to companies that must file statements with the Commission. However, because of the interaction between the Financial Accounting Standards Board and the SEC in developing reporting standards and because of the size and importance of the filing companies and their auditors, the SEC's influence extends to virtually all financial disclosure situations. Furthermore, because of the provisions in the 1934 Act governing proxy statements, the SEC has been granted regulatory power with respect to the preparation of annual reports to stockholders as well as reports to the SEC.

The Public Utility Holding Company Act of 1935 and the Foreign Corrupt Practices Act of 1977 give the SEC even broader authority over accounting practice than the 1933 or 1934 Acts. The SEC not only can specify the forms, procedures, and regulations to be used in filing forms with it, but also can dictate specific characteristics of the accounting system and its function within a registered company.

The other Acts administered by the SEC give added authority in accounting procedures as they relate to investment companies and broker-dealers.

Other Congressional Considerations. Another factor that may have led Congress to give the SEC broad power to regulate accounting was the recognized dependence of the investor on the opinion of the accountant. This dependence was noted years ago by Harry A. McDonald, a former Commissioner of the SEC, who said:

> One fact will always be dominant in shaping the course of accounting—the fact that whether directly or through his advisors, whether alone or through the medium of an agency like the SEC, the investor cannot help but look to the accountant.[1]

The idea of having government accountants perform the audits of registrants' financial statements pervaded Congress for a while, but the idea was finally set aside. Instead, Congress recognized the role of the independent public accountant and specified that financial statements filed with the SEC had to be certified by this independent agent.

SEC Authoritative Pronouncements

In exercising the broad regulatory authority described above, the SEC has relied primarily on generally accepted accounting principles as established by the accounting profession. The SEC has repeatedly stated that it considers principles, standards, and practices promulgated by the FASB as having substantial authoritative support—thus recognizing the FASB as the primary accounting standard-setting body since 1973. However, pursuant to its legal authority, the SEC can and does issue several types of authoritative pronouncements that clarify, modify, amend, or even supersede accounting principles established by the FASB. Four of the major SEC documents that give guidance for financial reporting principles, form and content are described in the next few paragraphs.

Regulation S-X is the principal source dictating the form and content of financial statements to be included in registration statements and financial reports filed with the SEC, but it does not contain all the SEC views on

---

1. Harry A. McDonald, "How Cooperation in Development of Accounting Principles by SEC and Profession Helps Investors," *The Journal of Accountancy,* 91 no. 3 (1951): 411–415.

accounting principles. Regulation S-X, codified in 1940, is continually being revised. Any accountant involved in SEC registration and reporting must be familiar with S-X and its current requirements.

Regulation S-K, Integrated Disclosure Rules, is a set of instructions for regulation of business and properties. It is similar in intent to Regulation S-X. As indicated, S-X prescribes the form and content of financial statements for SEC filings; S-K prescribes the requirements for nonfinancial statement information in SEC reporting. S-K also covers certain aspects of annual reports to shareholders.

In 1937, the SEC began issuing a series of releases intended to explain accounting procedures needing special treatment. These releases were known as Accounting Series Releases (ASRs). The ASRs also related to disciplinary sanctions imposed by the SEC. In 1982, after more than 300 ASRs had been issued, the SEC separated its releases into two series: (1) Financial Reporting Releases (FRRs) and (2) Accounting and Auditing Enforcement Releases (AAERs). In its first FRR, the SEC codified most of the previously issued ASRs that applied to financial matters. In effect, the codification superseded those ASRs that were nonenforcement-related. Currently, the FRRs are issued to keep registrant companies and accountants abreast of changing financial reporting requirements, and AAERs are issued when SEC enforcement activities are involved. Since the FRRs are used by the SEC to announce new rules, amend existing rules, and give its official position on matters relating to financial statements, FRRs are an important form of guidance for accountants.

In November 1975, the SEC, through its Division of Corporation Finance and Office of Chief Accountant, began issuing Staff Accounting Bulletins (SABs). The documents are not official rules or interpretations of the SEC like FRRs; instead, they represent interpretations and practices followed by the staff of the SEC in administering the disclosure requirements of the federal securities laws. However, many critics argue that the release of a SAB is a method of creating formal accounting policy—even though SABs are not "official" rules. For example, the release of SAB 101, "Revenue Recognition" in December of 1999 caused many firms to change their accounting practices and it forced the FASB to immediately issue authoritative literature to interpret the application of the SEC's guidance. (We discuss the events surrounding the release of SAB 101 later in this chapter.) Considering the perceived authoritative reputation of SABs, it is important for accountants and management to be familiar with them.

The involvement of the SEC in accounting practice has substantially influenced the considerable body of literature on accounting principles. It is also important to note that many of the SEC pronouncements carry the force of law, not just recommended adherence. Some examples of SEC pronouncements are discussed in this chapter.

SEC INFLUENCE ON FINANCIAL REPORTING, AUDITING AND CORPORATE GOVERNANCE PRACTICES

There are many areas in accounting and business in which the SEC has had a significant influence in the development of current practices. Obviously, not all such areas can be discussed. Specific illustrations presented in this chapter relate to (1) governing corporate boards of directors; (2) changes in auditing procedures; (3) regulation of the accounting and auditing profession; (4) new financial disclosure requirements for businesses; and (5) increased legal liabilities for managers, accountants, attorneys, and others.

Corporate Governance & the Board of Directors

The SEC historically has utilized financial reporting regulation as the principal means of protecting investors. Financial reporting provides an important accountability and stewardship in corporate governance. By requiring companies to comply with stringent reporting policies, the SEC has tried to enhance corporate governance and protect investors from fraud and deception. While the SEC continues to scrutinize accounting policies, it has also started to directly examine other aspects of corporate governance—especially boards of directors. With the financial reporting scandals of 2001–2003, the SEC has reexamined the crucial role of boards of directors in overseeing the actions of management and assuring the reliability of investor information.

Reflecting on the SEC's decision to strengthen corporate boards, Chairman William H. Donaldson sent a letter to the top officers of U.S. exchanges in March of 2003. Excerpts of the letter demonstrate the SEC's focus on improving corporate governance at a company's top levels:

> The recent corporate failures suffered by our nation have vividly shown the importance of accountability and sound governance

within shareholder-owned organizations. In response, there has been a broad examination of corporate governance practices throughout corporate America. Many organizations and individuals, including the U.S. Congress, the SEC, and myself have called for the establishment of corporate governance standards that reflect the highest commitment to ethics and transparency.

Doing so is essential to restoring a strong sense of investor confidence. It is now more important than ever that self-regulatory organizations be examples of good governance. Therefore, I ask you to engage in a review of your own corporate governance practices, including board structure and representation, and oversight of management policies and practices to ensure that they serve the public well. Bottom line, how do your governance practices reflect those expected of corporations traded on your market?[2]

Donaldson requested that each exchange send a complete review of the governance structure to the SEC for evaluation. The New York Stock Exchange (NYSE) received these instructions and responded with an initial report outlining areas of improvement—including a stated commitment to improve how compensation to executives would be determined.[3]

On August 27, 2003, after submitting the initial report, the NYSE announced a renegotiated contract with its Chairman and Chief Executive Officer Richard Grasso. The renegotiation included an outrageous payoff of $140 million for accrued savings and incentives. The staggering pay package prompted Donaldson to send a letter to the NYSE, stating his opinion of the payoff as follows:

In my view, the approval of Mr. Grasso's pay package raises serious questions regarding the effectiveness of the NYSE's current governance structure. I am especially concerned that the pay package was awarded before the Exchange completed its governance review, which has been pending since March. To better assess the steps that the NYSE has taken to date with respect to its

2. William H. Donaldson, *Letter to Exchange Officers Regarding SRO Corporate Governance*, 26 Mar. 2003. Accessed 17 Oct. 2003 <http://www.sec.gov/news/speech/spch032603whd.htm>.
3. William H. Donaldson, *Letter to NYSE Regarding NYSE Executive Compensation*, 2 Sep. 2003. Accessed 17 Oct. 2003 <http://www.sec.gov/news/speech/spch090203whd.htm>.

governance processes, we need full and complete information about the procedures and considerations that governed the award of Mr. Grasso's pay package.

The SEC immediately released this letter to the media, which heightened an already tense situation. Public opinion turned against Grasso, and demands for reforms were made. In order to calm investors and to quiet the uproar, the NYSE called a special board meeting and voted 13 to 7 in favor of Richard Grasso's removal.[4]

The NYSE quickly named an interim chairman, John S. Reed, who agreed to work for $1 regardless of his tenure.[5] More important than his salary, SEC chairman Donaldson gave his vote of confidence to the new chairman stating, "I am gratified that he is willing to take on this critical post. He is independent, experienced and has impeccable credentials, all of which will be crucial as he works with the NYSE Board to ensure the highest standards of governance."[6]

The replacement of Grasso demonstrates that the SEC does not have to apply direct sanctions or suspensions to alter the business landscape; suggestions and inquiries are often sufficient to cause the business community to move in the direction the SEC desires. The SEC's role in Richard Grasso's forced resignation sent a clear message to the business community regarding its commitment to proper corporate governance.

Changes in Auditing Standards & Procedures

The SEC, via the Sarbanes-Oxley Act of 2002 and the PCAOB, no longer allows the auditing profession to set "Generally Accepted Auditing Standards" (GAAS) for audits of public companies. For most of its history in the U.S., the auditing profession has attempted to carefully manage relations with the SEC. However, critics argue that this auditing self-regulation has been largely reactionary to the SEC and the scandal of the day. By reviewing specific cases, the reader will gain a greater appreciation for the SEC's proactive role in overseeing and regulating financial reporting and auditing.

---

4. Kate Kelly et al., "Grasso Quits Amid Pay Controversy," *The Wall Street Journal*, 18 Sep. 2003, sec A: 1.
5. Laurie P. Cohen, "NYSE Names John S. Reed Acting Chairman," *The Wall Street Journal*, 22 Sep. 2003, sec C: 1.
6. Kelly, op. cit.

The McKesson and Robbins Case. The case of *McKesson and Robbins* (1940) shows how an initial SEC review led to subsequent action by the accounting profession and resulted in revised and updated auditing standards.[7] In this well-known case, several million dollars of fictitious receivables and inventories were included on the financial statements certified by the company's independent auditors. The SEC investigated and found that the auditing procedures followed were not sufficient, even though they were in accordance with GAAS at that time. In response, the accounting profession took action in establishing additional standards that required auditors to observe inventories and confirm receivable balances with third parties. In view of the responsive action by the accounting profession, the SEC decided to continue to allow the profession to develop auditing procedures, subject to its oversight.

The Yale Express Case. Another example of SEC action leading to subsequent revision of auditing standards by the accounting profession is the now well-publicized *Yale Express* case.[8] In this case, the SEC filed an *amicus curiae* brief stating that accountants have a duty to disclose subsequent discovery of material error existing at the report date in financial statements that were previously certified. In 1971, this action led the AICPA to the issuance of a Statement on Auditing Procedure (SAP) No. 47 "Subsequent Events" (now AU Sections 560 as codified in Statements on Auditing Standards No. 1), which detailed the procedures to be followed by auditors upon subsequent discovery of events affecting their opinions on financial statements previously certified.

Financial Statement Materiality. In 1998, the then Chairman of the SEC, Arthur Levitt, spoke about the "Numbers Game" of earnings management that he alleged many in corporate America were playing.

> Today, I'd like to talk to you about another widespread, but too little-challenged custom: earnings management. This process has evolved over the years into what can best be characterized as a game among market participants. A game that, if not addressed soon, will have adverse consequences for America's financial

---

7. *Dennis v. McKesson and Robbins, Inc.* No. 66. U.S.D.C. District of Conn. 1938.
8. *Fischer v. Klet,* 266 F. Supp. 180 S.D.N.Y. 1967.

reporting system. A game that runs counter to the very principles behind our market's strength and success.

Increasingly, I have become concerned that the motivation to meet Wall Street earnings expectations may be overriding common sense business practices. Too many corporate managers, auditors, and analysts are participants in a game of nods and winks. In the zeal to satisfy consensus earnings estimates and project a smooth earnings path, wishful thinking may be winning the day over faithful representation.[9]

Levitt went on to describe five practices of accountants that amounted to accounting "Hocus Pocus;" this list included the misuse of materiality. To remedy the problem of systematic misuse of materiality and the other accounting "games" being played, Levitt prescribed:

Immediate and coordinated action: technical rule changes by the regulators and standard setters to improve the transparency of financial statements; enhanced oversight of the financial reporting process by those entrusted as the shareholders' guardians; and nothing less than a fundamental cultural change on the part of corporate management as well as the whole financial community. This action plan represents a cooperative public-private sector effort.[10]

As part of the action plan, Levitt encouraged the FASB to work for a prompt resolution of their projects, but he didn't stop there. Levitt stated the SEC would get directly involved in improving the situation by increasing its efforts to detect abuses, particularly for firms that announce restructuring of liability reserves, major write-offs, or other practices that appear to manage earnings.

Not only did the SEC increase its effort to detect abuses, but it issued statements to curtail exploitation of accounting rules and concepts. One of these statements, SAB 99, "Materiality," expresses the views of the staff that, "exclusive reliance on certain quantitative benchmarks to assess materiality in preparing financial statements and performing audits of those financial

---

9. Arthur Levitt, "The 'Numbers Game,' " 28 Sep. 1998. Accessed 17 Oct. 2003 <http://www.sec.gov/news/speech/speecharchive/1998/spch220.txt>.
10. Ibid.

statements is inappropriate; misstatements are not immaterial simply because they fall beneath a numerical threshold."[11]

SAB 99 did not introduce new regulations, but instead reiterated the importance of several previous rules. Particularly, SAB 99 emphasized the importance of considering both "quantitative" and "qualitative" factors in determining materiality.[12]

The accounting profession was quick to pay heed to the bulletin; notwithstanding, it was issued as an opinion of the SEC staff. The AICPA quickly updated Practice Alert No. 94-1, "Dealing with Audit Differences," which urged auditors to consider SAB 99 when calculating materiality.[13] The practice alert was followed by new Statements on Auditing Standards (SAS) No. 89, "Audit Adjustments," and No. 90, "Audit Committee Communication," which included concepts from the SEC's bulletin.

The SEC released SAB 99 because it perceived a lack of action by the accounting profession. The release caused the accounting profession to immediately focus on the issue of materiality and take steps to curtail abuses by companies in managing earnings while claiming that these abuses were "not material." By raising the issue first in a speech and then in a staff bulletin, the SEC caused the auditing standard setters to quickly move in the direction the SEC desired.

Regulation of Financial Reporting

The SEC utilizes three primary tools to regulate the financial reporting process: (1) standard setting, (2) sanctions, and (3) suspensions. The first method is used to deter the release of deficient information while the later two serve to punish violators.

Standard Setting. For nearly 70 years the SEC served as a watchdog over the auditing and attestation functions of the accounting profession, while delegating the authority to set policies and standards in these areas to the profession itself. However, through the Sarbanes-Oxley Act of 2002, the

---

11. United States, Securities and Exchange Commission, "Staff Accounting Bulletin: No. 99 – Materiality." 13 Aug. 1999. Accessed 17 Oct. 2003 <http://www.sec.gov/interps/account/sab99.htm>.
12. Ibid.
13. American Institute of Certified Public Accountants, "Practice Alert No. 94-1 Dealing with Audit Differences," 1 Dec. 1999. Accessed 17 Oct. 2003 <http://www.aicpa.org/members/div/secps/ lit/practice/941.htm>.

establishment of the Public Company Accounting Oversight Board ended auditing self-regulation.

The PCAOB is a private-sector, non-profit corporation enterprise that attempts to ensure that the interests of investors are protected.[14] Although the Board is a "private-sector" corporation, the SEC appointed the initial chairperson and members of the Board; the SEC also gave the Board power to raise revenue by requiring firms to fund the existence of the Board. The obligatory roll of funding the auditing standard setters helps the PCAOB fulfill the responsibility of the Board to protect investors (a detailed description of the PCAOB is contained in Chapter 3).

The Board faces the daunting task of restoring investor confidence in financial accounting reports. William McDonough, the first chairman of the PCAOB, shared his vision of how to restore lost credibility: "I see the job of the PCAOB as providing guidance in a constructive manner and, when necessary, to be a tough overseer to protect the public's interests and assure that any inappropriate behavior is ended."[15] The Board has two principal means to provide guidance and discipline to the auditing field: (1) issue new auditing standards, and (2) inspect public accounting firms that provide audit reports to publicly held companies.[16]

In April 2003, the PCAOB voted to adopt the auditing standards promulgated by the AICPA's Auditing Standards Board on an interim basis. In March 2004, the PCAOB released its first standard, "An Audit of Internal Control Over Financial Reporting Performed in Conjunction with an Audit of Financial Statements." The purpose of this new standard is to provide guidance on the attestation of internal controls as required by Sarbanes-Oxley 404.

The SEC's switch to a government-appointed standard setter rather than letting the profession regulate itself is a landmark shift. Time will tell if the shift results in standards, working practices, and discipline that prove more effective than did self-regulation.

Suspensions and Sanctions. Although the SEC has delegated auditing standard setting authority to the PCAOB, the SEC still maintains a powerful

---

14. David Cottrell, and Steven Glover, "Finding Auditors Liable for Fraud," *The CPA Journal,.* 67 no. 7 (1997): 14–21.

15. William McDonough, "Statement of William McDonough," 15 Apr. 2003. Accessed 17 Oct. 2003 <http://www.sec.gov/news/extra/mcdonough41503.htm >.

16. United States, *Sarbanes Oxley Act of 2002,* Section 103(a)1 and Section 104(a) respectively.

regulatory role through suspensions and sanctions. The SEC can suspend an auditor or an entire auditing firm if they are found to

- Not have the necessary qualifications.
- Be engaged in unethical behavior.
- Have willfully violated any of the Federal Securities laws or rules.
- Have exhibited "improper professional conduct."
- Have been convicted of a felony or a misdemeanor involving moral turpitude.[17]

Sanctions and suspensions can result in heavy fines, severe loss of clientele, or loss of the privilege to appear and practice before the SEC. Concurrent with the writing of this text, the SEC is recommending to an administrative-law judge to suspend an entire firm for the first time since 1975.[18] The SEC is seeking a six-month suspension that would prevent Ernst & Young from accepting new public-company audit clients; in a 120-page brief the SEC asserts that "E&Y's 'independence control system' is unworthy to be so called."[19] These allegations stem from Ernst & Young's co-development and promotion of PeopleSoft software while E&Y was PeopleSoft's auditor.[20]

Ernst and Young "vehemently disagrees" with the SEC's accusations and presents as evidence a report issued by a group appointed by the SEC to examine E&Y's independence policies. The report stated that E&Y's policies "were effectively designed and implemented."[21] Regardless of the outcome of this situation, the SEC is demonstrating its power and its willingness to enforce the rules.

Suspensions and sanctions are not limited to accountants and their firms. Between 2000 and 2002, the SEC suspended 28 companies. The SEC has the power to suspend trading in any stock for up to 10 days, and the SEC utilizes this power in extreme cases in which the Commission believes that the public information regarding the security is inaccurate or

17. United States, Securities and Exchange Commission, "Rules of Practice: Rule 102(e)." Accessed 17 Oct. 2003 <http://www.sec.gov/about/rulesofpractice.shtml#102>.
18. Cassell Bryan-Low, and Jonathan Weil, "Ernst Controls are Faulted by SEC." *The Wall Street Journal Europe*, 2 June 2003, sec M: 4.
19. Ibid.
20. Ameet Sachdev, "Regulators Still Drawing the Line on Auditors," *Chicago Tribune*, 7 Oct. 2003: 1.
21. Bryan-Low, op. cit. M: 4.

that the public information regarding the security is inaccurate or inadequate. For instance, the SEC suspended trading HealthSouth in March of 2003, the day after the FBI searched HealthSouth's headquarters as part of an investigation into possible accounting fraud.[22] Suspensions damage a company's reputation and limit the company's ability to raise money through the capital market. Sanctions have been an effective way for the SEC to demonstrate its powerful regulatory role to all involved. An example of SEC sanctioning power was the SEC's ability to negotiate a $1.4 billion dollar settlement with the major Wall Street brokerages in April of 2003. The settlement came at the conclusion of an extensive SEC investigation into allegations that the brokerages provided the public with misleading research to increase demand for investment banking deals.[23]

Disclosure Requirements

An essential objective of the SEC is to provide full and fair disclosure of financial and other information for investors. Therefore, it should not be surprising that the SEC has had a significant impact on the reporting requirements of businesses. Often at the urging or insistence of the SEC, requirements for both the amount of information disclosed and the extent of detail provided are increasing. For example in Chapter 3 we noted that additional disclosures are mandated by the Sarbanes-Oxley Act. To shed additional light on the subject of disclosure, this section examines the recent legislation against selective disclosure and insider trading (for additional disclosure information relative to Sarbanes-Oxley, please refer to Chapter 3).

Selective Disclosure and Insider Trading.   For years small investors have claimed that large investors have an advantage in the stock market; a complaint based on the idea that large investors receive tips or insider information before the rest of the public. In August of 2000, traders pointed to the large stock price fluctuations of companies such as Apple, Clorox, and Abercrombie & Fitch, the fluctuations purportedly caused by "information exchanged at a closed-door company meeting with their

22. HealthSouth, "HealthSouth Issues Statement on Federal Investigation," 19 Mar. 2003. Accessed 22 Mar. 2004 <http://www.prnewswire.com>. Also Greg Farrell, "HealthSouth, CEO Face Charges on Earnings," *USA Today*. 19 Mar. 2003. Accessed 22 Mar. 2004 <http://www.usatoday.com/ money/industries/health/2003-03-19-healthsouth_x.htm>.
23. "Wall Street to Pay the Piper," *www.CBSNews.com* 2 May 2003. Accessed 23 Mar. 2004 <http://www.cbsnews.com/stories/2003/05/02/national/main552049.shtml>.

more-favored peers."[24] To combat this perceived problem, the SEC issued Regulation Fair Disclosure (FD), which requires that when an issuer or person acting on its behalf discloses material nonpublic information to certain enumerated persons, it must make public disclosure of that information within 24 hours."[25]

Regulation FD facilitates the mission of the SEC, "to protect investors and maintain the integrity of the securities markets."[26] Individuals or companies that violate Regulation FD, either by profiting from "tips" or by disseminating "tips," face the possibility of a cease-and-desist order, an injunction, and/or civil money penalties.

After a year of limited enforcement, the SEC intensified its enforcement of Regulation FD. Richard J. Kogan, the former chief executive of pharmaceutical-developer Schering-Plough, allegedly tipped off large investors when he "provided a litany of negative information, in what he said and in his manner, in meetings with the institutional investors."[27] Kogan met with large investors and forecasted that Schering-Plough would not meet analysts' earnings expectations, while at the same time portraying a positive forecast to the general public. The SEC, upon hearing of the unfair dissemination of information, began an investigation of Schering-Plough based on Regulation FD. As part of a settlement, Schering-Plough and Kogan neither admitted nor denied the accusations, but did agree to pay a $1 million dollar penalty as a company and Kogan agreed to a $50,000 personal fine.[28]

Development of Accounting Principles

The SEC's policy has been to allow the accounting profession to play a major role in the development of generally accepted accounting principles. In 1938, ASR No. 4 stated a twofold requirement for financial statements. First, to be accepted by the SEC at all, financial statements must be prepared

24. Homan Jenkins, "Smart Investors Let Others Do the Work." *The Wall Street Journal,* 16 Aug. 2000, sec A: 23.

25. United States, Securities and Exchange Commission, "Final Rule: Selective Disclosure and Insider Trading," Release No. 33-7881, 15 Aug. 2000.

26. United States, Securities and Exchange Commission, "The Investor's Advocate: How the SEC Protects Investors and Maintains Market Integrity," 21 July 2003. Accessed 23 Mar. 2004 <http://www.sec.gov/about/whatwedo.shtml>.

27. Floyd Norris, "SEC Penalizes Schering-Plough over a Fair Disclosure Violation," *New York Times.* 10 Sep. 2003, sec C: 1.

28. Ibid.

in accordance with accounting principles which have "substantial authoritative support." Second, if the SEC disagrees with the registrant, and if the accounting principles used have substantial authoritative support, the SEC will accept footnotes to the statements in lieu of correcting the statements to the SEC view, provided the SEC has not previously expressed its opinion on the matter in published material.

Two points are critical to an understanding of the relationship of the SEC and accounting principles. First, the SEC reserves the right explicitly (which it would have anyway under its general powers) to rule against a registrant even if it follows principles having substantial authoritative support. Second, the SEC reserves the right to determine which principles have substantial authoritative support.

Government Involvement. The SEC has delegated power to set accounting standards to three different organizations through its history—first the Committee on Accounting Procedure (CAP), then the Accounting Principles Board (APB), and currently the Financial Accounting Standards Board (FASB). Each of these organizations has worked to produce Generally Accepted Accounting Principles (GAAP). The FASB received its official vote of confidence from the SEC in 1973 through ASR No. 150. In addition to stating the FASB's authority to institute rules, this statement expresses the SEC's hope that "the expertise, energy and resources of the accounting profession" would "provide leadership in establishing and improving accounting principles."[29] Despite this policy of encouraging the profession to take the lead in developing principles, the SEC has not always expressed unqualified confidence in the profession's ability and performance.

Robert Herdman, former Chief Accountant of the SEC, outlined before Congress what the SEC has been trying to do for several years in relation to the FASB:

Concerns have arisen that the FASB is not being as responsive as it should be. Even before the recent events, the SEC staff called upon the FASB to work with us to address concerns about timeliness, transparency, and complexity. Specifically, we asked the FASB to address the following concerns:

---

29. Accounting Series Release No. 150 (December 20, 1973), "Statement of Policy on the Establishment and Improvement of Accounting Principles and Standards," *SEC Docket*, Vol. 3, No. 7 (January 2, 1974): 276 (notes omitted). Codification of Financial Reporting Policies, ¶101, *Federal Securities Law Reports* (Chicago: Commerce Clearing House), ¶72,921.

- The current standard-setting process is too cumbersome and slow.
- Much of the recent FASB guidance is rule based and focuses on a check-the-box mentality that inhibits transparency.
- Much of the recent FASB guidance is too complex.[30]

This quote reveals how the SEC had been seeking for reforms even before the recent accounting scandals. The accounting failures served only to increase the SEC's pressure on the FASB to implement changes. Examination of two examples of how the SEC worked with the FASB before the recent accounting scandals and one example after the scandals provides insights into how policy making decisions might be made in the future.

Accounting for Stock Options. One of the most interesting examples of the SEC's interactions with the FASB in the development of accounting principles is seen in the creation of rules governing the accounting for stock options.

Many companies, especially start-up companies with limited cash resources, choose to give employees stock options instead of cash compensation. The debate over how to account for stock options has a long history beginning in 1972. The accounting standard-setting body at the time, the Accounting Principles Board, issued Accounting Principles Board Opinion (APB) No. 25, which dealt with stock options. APB Opinion No. 25 set forth the "intrinsic value method" of reporting stock option compensation expense. Under this approach, a company did not need to expense stock option grants if their exercise price was equal to or greater than the market price on the day the shares were granted. Most companies would not immediately recognize an expense under this method. In March of 1994, the FASB held hearings on its first proposed accounting rule that would require companies to expense stock options and would result in many companies reporting much-lower net income than they otherwise

---

30. Robert Herdman, "Testimony Concerning the Roles of the SEC and the FASB in Establishing GAAP," 14 May 2002. Accessed 17 Oct. 2003
<http://www.sec.gov/news/testimony/051402tsrkh.htm>.

would.[31] Members of the FASB were unprepared for the stiff opposition that came from the business community and Congress. One senator from California stated, "The FASB stock option proposal would be damaging to many companies in our Nation . . . It would be very damaging to California's nascent economic recovery . . . If we need to legislate accounting rules, I am not going to walk away from that fight . . . ."[32]

Not surprisingly, much of the strongest opposition to the FASB's proposal came from Silicon Valley, home to many high-tech start-ups. Technology companies commonly rely heavily on stock option compensation both as a means to attract and to retain quality employees. These technology companies also tend to rely heavily on outside financing and realize they would not appear as attractive to investors if they were to expense their stock options. The technology companies and the business community in general had powerful allies against the FASB's proposed rule in Congress. One of these, Senator Joseph Lieberman of Connecticut, pushed a resolution through the Senate opposing the FASB's proposal on an 88-9 vote. He also led a coalition that tried to strip the FASB of its powers, but failed.

Some influential businesspeople argued that stock options should be expensed, however. Warren Buffet, president of Berkshire Hathaway, stated the following in a 1993 letter to shareholders:

> If options aren't a form of compensation, what are they? If compensation isn't an expense, what is it? And if expenses shouldn't go into the calculation of earnings, where in the world should they go?[33]

In the end, however, the political pressure proved too great. The SEC and its Chairman, Arthur Levitt, sided with Congress and the business world. Levitt urged and persuaded the FASB to surrender (though years later Levitt would admit this was a mistake). As a result, the FASB finally

31. Brian Milner, "Stock Options Expensing is Still a Hard Sell in U.S." *GlobeInvestor.com.* 15 Mar. 2004. Accessed 22 Mar. 2004
<http://www.globeinvestor.com/servlet/ArticleNews/story/GAM/20040315/RMILN15>.
32. *Congressional Record—Senate,* 3 May 1994, pp. S5035-S5036. Quoted in Stephan A. Zeff and Bala G. Dharan, *Readings and Notes on Financial Accounting: Issues and Controversies,* 5th ed. (New York: McGraw-Hill, 1997).
33. Berkshire Hathaway, *Annual Report—1993.*

promulgated SFAS 123 in 1995, which encourages, but does not require, the expensing of stock options.

Companies such as Coca-Cola, Amazon.com, Bank One, and *The Washington Post* have voluntarily expensed stock options. The decision to expense stock options is in response to the FASB's urging as well as a desire by these companies to signal to the marketplace that they are "high quality" and "transparent" reporters of financial information. At Apple Computer's 2003 annual meeting, a shareholder proposal on expensing options received a majority vote, the first time this has happened at a major technology company.[34]

Just like Apple Computer shareholders, many other business people are calling for more transparent financial reporting—including the mandatory expensing of stock options. At the time of this writing, the FASB is once again considering requiring the expensing of stock options, and this time the SEC appears to be lending crucial support.

This example shows the political environment in which accounting standards are established. The SEC oversees the FASB's efforts and sometimes overrules their decisions based on political pressure or the SEC's own opinions about what is best for the financial reporting process and for enhancing accountability.

Revenue Recognition. Another example of the SEC influencing the development of accounting policies is with rules regarding revenue recognition.

Revenues are usually the largest single item in the financial statements, and arguably one of the most important numbers to investors. Notable frauds committed recently by Sunbeam and Enron involved the overstatement of revenues, a technique found to be used in over half the frauds committed from 1987 to 1997.[35]

The FASB has tried to deal with the issue of revenue recognition for many years. In 1984 the FASB released Statement of Financial Accounting Concept (SFAC) No. 5, which sets two general criteria for revenue to be recognized: (1) the revenue must be realized or realizable and (2) the

---

34. Howard Stock, "FASB's Options Expensing Rule Planned for Next Year," *Investor Relations Business.* 12 May 2003, P.1.

35. Mark Beasley et al., "Fraudulent Financial Reporting: 1987–1997 An Analysis of U.S. Public Companies," 30 Nov. 1999. Accessed 17 Oct. 2003
<http://bear.cba.ufl.edu/hackenbrack/acg5637/FFR.htm>.

revenue must be earned. In order to be recognized as revenue and included on the income statement, a transaction must meet both of these criteria. While a simple concept in theory, the FASB, SEC, AICPA, and the Emerging Issues Task Force (EITF) have all issued multiple pronouncements on this topic, which can be extremely tricky in application.

In then-SEC Chairman Arthur Levitt's famous speech, the "Numbers Game," Levitt indicated that many in corporate America were playing tricks to manage earnings. The most common trick was the improper recognition of revenues. Levitt compared the inappropriate recognition of revenues to a bottle of wine.

> Think about a bottle of fine wine. You wouldn't pop the cork on that bottle before it was ready. But some companies are doing this with their revenue—recognizing it before a sale is complete, before the product is delivered to a customer, or at a time when the customer still has options to terminate, void, or delay the sale.[36]

To solve the early revenue recognition problem, Levitt encouraged the FASB to work for a prompt resolution of their projects, but he didn't stop there. Levitt stated that the "SEC staff will immediately consider interpretive accounting guidance on the do's and don'ts of revenue recognition. The staff will also determine whether recently published standards for the software industry can be applied to other service companies."[37]

In 1999, the SEC issued Staff Accounting Bulletin (SAB) 101, "Revenue Recognition." SAB 101 elaborates on one of the two criteria the FASB had provided in SFAS No. 5—what it means for a sale to be realized or realizable. In SAB 101 the SEC provided four criteria and thirteen mini-cases to illustrate their interpretation of a realized or realizable sale.

The SEC's action was a response to a perceived problem in the accounting rules. Immediately after the release of SAB 101, the FASB's Emerging Issues Task Force issued interpretative guidance on SAB 101. The immediate response demonstrates the SEC's direct impact on GAAP. A year after SAB 101 was released, the FASB added a project to its agenda to develop a comprehensive Statement of Financial Accounting Standard (SFAS) dealing with revenue recognition. The FASB explained that it added

36. Levitt, op. cit.
37. Ibid.

a policy on revenue recognition to its agenda because of concerns it has with the SEC issuing SAB 101:

> Some criticize SAB 101 on the basis that the criteria in SOP 97-2 were developed for a particular industry and that broader application of those criteria was neither contemplated nor intended . . . Others note that a SAB is designed to provide the SEC staff's interpretive responses and not to change generally accepted accounting principles (GAAP). For that reason, SABs are issued without an invitation for comment. Critics argue that SAB 101 has in fact changed GAAP by promulgating changes in industry practice without the full due process and deliberation that characterize the FASB's decision-making process. Moreover, the guidance in SAB 101 applies only to SEC registrants. Nonetheless, the work done in developing and implementing SAB 101 has focused attention on revenue recognition issues and will be very useful in this project.[38]

Pro Forma Statements. At times the SEC has "overruled" accounting rules proposed by the FASB, such as in the stock options example. Other times the SEC provides guidance that can be used until the FASB provides official standards, as demonstrated by SAB 101. On occasion, the SEC creates accounting rules. Such is the case with recent SEC rules on pro forma statements.

Pro forma statements are non-GAAP descriptions of financial statements that have one or more assumptions or hypothetical conditions built into the data. An example might be a company reporting on what its income would have been if it had taken a particular course of action. Other examples of pro forma information are net income ignoring unusual or non-recurring expenses and Earnings Before Interest, Taxes, Depreciation, and Amortization (EBITDA). In the late 1990s and early 2000s, hundreds of companies, particularly start-up technology companies, issued pro forma earnings reports in press releases, which almost always presented the company in the best possible light. Pro forma releases are believed to have

---

38. Financial Accounting Standards Board, "Project Updates: Revenue Recognition," 30 Sep. 2003. Accessed 17 Oct. 2003
<http://www.fasb.org/project/revenue_recognition.shtml#history>.

contributed to the "irrational exuberance" observed in the stock market during that period. In 2001, as Chief Accountant of the SEC, Lynn Turner dubbed pro forma press releases "EBS," or "Everything but Bad Stuff," releases because companies tended to highlight only positive financial information and frequently refer to normal operating expenses as "unusual."[39] Companies defended their use of pro forma information by asserting the following:

- They reported their GAAP financial information to the SEC anyway,
- GAAP includes irrelevant non-cash and non-recurring expenses, and
- GAAP doesn't provide insight into a company's future based on specific assumptions or projections.

Even though it was not GAAP, companies were able to issue pro forma information in their press releases because SEC authority did not extend to press releases. Because no rules existed relating to releases of pro forma information, companies had the freedom to present their financial information however they desired. As a result, there was little consistency in pro forma reporting across companies or even year-to-year for the same company.

Although the SEC generally had little or no authority to prevent companies from disseminating pro forma information to the public, the SEC brought an enforcement action against Trump Hotels & Casino Resorts Inc. for giving misleading pro forma information in its third-quarter 1999 earnings release. Trump's release cited pro forma figures that indicated positive results from operations but failed to mention those results were largely due to an unusual one-time gain rather than operations. Stephen Cutler, Director of the SEC's Division of Enforcement said, "In this case, the method of presenting the pro forma numbers and the positive spin the Company put on them were materially misleading. The case starkly

39. Lynn Turner, "Audit Committees: A Roadmap for Establishing Accountability," 10 Mar. 2001. Accessed 24 Mar. 2004
<http://www.sec.gov/news/speech/speecharchive/2001speech.shtml>.

illustrates how pro forma numbers can be used deceptively and the mischief that they can cause."[40]

In response to the Sarbanes-Oxley Act, the SEC adopted Regulation G in January 2003, relating to pro forma and other non-GAAP press releases. Regulation G requires public companies that disclose or release pro forma financial measures to also present a reconciliation of the pro forma information to the most directly comparable GAAP financial measure. In adopting Regulation G, the SEC hopes to impose discipline on the disclosure of pro forma information to prevent investors from being misled.

The SEC did not attempt to influence the FASB to create new rules governing pro forma numbers. Instead, the SEC immediately acted to create regulation it believed would mitigate the problem.

The examples in this section illustrate the fundamental shift in the SEC's belief in accounting self-regulation over the past several years. The SEC still allows the FASB to develop accounting rules, but the SEC will continue to influence accounting standards in a variety of ways, from encouraging and persuading the FASB to directly creating accounting policy.

Changing Environment

The SEC's interaction with the accounting profession and the business community is a dynamic process. The relationship depends on many factors, including the political and economic climate and the philosophies of both the Chairman and the Chief Accountant of the SEC. There have been periods of great activity and SEC involvement and other times when relatively little interaction between the SEC and accounting policy setters has occurred. In recent years, the SEC has shifted from "behind the scenes" oversight and persuasion to a more active roll in providing guidance or policy to the accounting profession. If, in the future, the SEC believes that the accounting profession is not properly addressing challenges and opportunities, it seems clear that the SEC will assertively influence accounting and auditing practices and standards as a means of meeting its responsibilities under the federal securities acts.

---

40. United States, Securities and Exchange Commission, "SEC Brings First Pro Forma Financial Reporting Case," 16 Jan. 2003. Accessed 18 Oct. 2003. <http://www.sec.gov/news/headlines/trumphotels.htm>.

SUMMARY

The SEC has significantly influenced the accounting profession and the business community. The SEC's influence is an important factor in determining generally accepted accounting principles and auditing standards as well as business practices. Until 2003, both accounting and auditing standards were set by private-sector organizations, with SEC oversight. In 2003, auditing standards for public companies was moved from the private sector to the Public Company Accounting Oversight Board (PCAOB), a quasi-governmental agency under the supervision of the SEC. The Sarbanes-Oxley Act established the PCAOB, and the SEC selected its board members. The SEC has direct oversight responsibilities and approves PCAOB standards before they are released.

While accounting standards for both private and public companies are still promulgated by the FASB in the private sector, the accounting profession and standards setters must demonstrate continuous improvement, integrity, and a willingness to take tough stands in a timely fashion in order to maintain the privilege of establishing accounting standards.

For public companies, the SEC still has the last word for both accounting and auditing standards via the authority conferred by Congress. In the wake of the recent accounting scandals, the SEC has been more assertive in influencing corporate governance and financial reporting practices and standards.

DISCUSSION QUESTIONS

1. Why has the SEC been given such broad statutory power in relation to accounting principles and procedures?

2. How was the SEC granted this power? Trace the events.

3. What are the Financial Reporting Releases and Accounting and Auditing Enforcement Releases? What is the purpose of FRRs? How do FRRs differ from SABs (Staff Accounting Bulletins)?

4. Why is the formation of the PCAOB historically significant? Why is this seen as an historic change for accountants and auditors of public companies?

5. Consider some of the instances in which the SEC has exerted influence on auditing standards and the significance of these influences. In what ways can the SEC influence corporate governance, financial reporting, and auditing?

6. How has the SEC generally elected to fulfill its responsibilities with regard to accounting standards? What are the strengths and the weaknesses of this tendency?

7. What seems to be the current trend of the SEC action in regard to accounting principles?

Index